MAKERS
of the
MUSLIM
WORLD

Beshir Agha

"It is clearly written, and simplifies without condescending or sacrificing the research that has gone into its preparation."

DR VIRGINIA AKSAN, ASSOCIATE PROFESSOR OF HISTORY, McMASTER UNIVERSITY

SELECTION OF TITLES IN THE MAKERS OF THE MUSLIM WORLD SERIES

Series editor: Patricia Crone,
Institute for Advanced Study, Princeton

'Abd al-Malik, Chase F. Robinson
Abd al-Rahman III, Maribel Fierro
Abu Nuwas, Philip Kennedy
Ahmad ibn Hanbal, Christopher Melchert
Ahmad Riza Khan Barelwi, Usha Sanyal
Al-Ma'mun, Michael Cooperson
Al-Mutanabbi, Margaret Larkin
Amir Khusraw, Sunil Sharma
Fazlallah Astarabadi and the Hurufis, Shazad Bashir
Ibn 'Arabi, William C. Chittick
Ibn Fudi, Ahmad Dallal
Ikhwan al-Safa', Godefroid de Callataÿ
Shaykh Mufid, Tamima Bayhom-Daou

For current information and details of other books in the series, please visit www.oneworld-publications.com/

MAKERS
of the
MUSLIM
WORLD

Beshir Agha

Chief Eunuch of the Ottoman Imperial Harem

JANE HATHAWAY

ONEWORLD
ACADEMIC

BESHIR AGHA

A Oneworld Book
First published by Oneworld Publications, 2005
Reprinted, 2019

A CIP record for this title is available
from the British Library

ISBN 978-1-85168-390-1
eISBN 978-1-78074-195-6

Typeset by Sparks, Oxford
Cover and text designed by Design Deluxe
Printed and Bound in Great Britain
by Clays Ltd, Elcograf S.p.A.

Oneworld Publications
10 Bloomsbury Street
London, WC1B 3SR
England

FOR BOB, BESHIR, AND STELLA

CONTENTS

ACKNOWLEDGMENTS

I would like to thank Dr Tijana Krstic of the University of Michigan for her help in procuring a publication dealing with the Eyüp Cemetery in Istanbul, and Professor George Junne of the University of Northern Colorado for supplying some helpful photographs of Beshir Agha's religious complex outside Topkapı Palace. I also thank Patricia Crone for her meticulous editorial work and many helpful insights.

NOTE ON TRANSLITERATION

I have made every attempt to render Turkish and Arabic names in anglicized form (in the case of Turkish names, using *j* instead of *c*, *ch* instead of *ç*, and *sh* instead of *ş*, for example). I have, however, retained the Turkish undotted "ı," which denotes a sound roughly equivalent to the short "u" in "put," as well as *ö* (similar to *œ* in French), *ü* (similar to *u* in French), and the soft "g" (ğ), similar to the "g" in *espagnol*. I have omitted long vowel signs from transliterations of Arabic, except in the cases of book titles and titles of certain offices, where I have followed the transliteration guidelines of the *International Journal of Middle East Studies*. Most Muslim names in this study are rendered in Romanized Ottoman Turkish forms (thus, Mehmed instead of Muhammad, except in the case of the Prophet, and Ahmed instead of Ahmad) in view of the fact that most of the figures in this work were Turkish-speaking Ottoman subjects.

INTRODUCTION

This is a biography of el-Hajj Beshir Agha, who held the post of chief eunuch of the imperial harem of the Ottoman Empire from 1717 to 1746 and was arguably the most powerful occupant of that office in Ottoman history. Although he was not a warrior for Islam, a great theologian or jurist, or a mystic-saint, Beshir Agha left his mark on the Ottoman brand of orthodox Sunni Islam of the Hanafi legal rite. In so doing, he epitomized the religious and intellectual role of the chief harem eunuch, who, so far from presiding over a den of iniquity, as outmoded Orientalist stereotypes would have it, functioned as a proponent of Sunni Muslim tenets and values.

THE OTTOMAN EMPIRE

Starting as a tiny Turkish principality in northwestern Anatolia (the peninsula comprising the bulk of modern-day Turkey), the Ottoman Empire expanded dramatically during the fourteenth and early fifteenth centuries, conquering the Balkans from the Byzantine Empire and the rest of Anatolia from rival Turkish principalities before finally taking the Byzantine capital of Constantinople in 1453, thus bringing the ancient Byzantine Empire to an end. In the early sixteenth century, the Ottomans added most of the Arab lands to their domains. At its height, during the reign of the legendary sultan Süleyman I (r. 1520–66, known in Western Europe as "the Magnificent"), the Ottoman Empire stretched from Hungary in the north to Ethiopia in the south and from the borders of Morocco in the west to the borders of Iran in the east. By Beshir Agha's time, the empire had begun to lose territory in the west and north to the Habsburg emperors of Austria and Central Europe, as well as to a newly expansionist

Russia. Nonetheless, the Ottoman Empire remained a power to be reckoned with.

Ottoman Islam

The Islam that the Ottomans espoused was Sunni, as distinct from the Shi'ism of the rival Safavid Empire, which took over Iran in 1501. (The differences between the two sects will be discussed in more detail in chapter 6.) Sunni Islam recognizes four schools, or "rites," of legal interpretation; these evolved during the eighth and ninth centuries, and break down largely along regional lines. They differ chiefly over rituals, such as washing before prayer, and personal status matters, such as divorce and inheritance. The Ottomans adhered to the Hanafi school and were virtually unique among Islamic empires in making it their official imperial rite. While they did not attempt to impose Hanafism on all their Muslim subjects, they did appoint chief judges and other key religious officials of the Hanafi rite throughout their empire.

At the same time, the Ottoman brand of Sunni, Hanafi Islam was historically tolerant of, and even favorably disposed toward, the Muslim mystical, or sufi, orders, which had become widespread during the twelfth and thirteenth centuries. Virtually since the empire's inception, certain orders had been close to the Ottoman court. Beshir Agha, as we shall see, espoused and promoted both Hanafism and sufism.

THE CHIEF HAREM EUNUCH'S INFLUENCE

By the end of the sixteenth century, the chief harem eunuch had become one of the most influential figures in the Ottoman Empire, at some times second only to the sultan and the grand vizier (a prime minister equivalent), at others second to none for all practical purposes. He oversaw the early education of the crown princes within the harem precinct of the imperial palace, and was thus able to mold the religious and intellectual predispositions of future sultans. He himself received a thorough-going Islamic education in the palace; this would constitute the foundation of his future intellectual and religious development just as the books he studied in the palace school would constitute the foundation of his future library or libraries.

Chief harem eunuchs were legendary book-collectors, and Beshir Agha was perhaps the most legendary of them all. The several libraries that he founded during his lifetime boasted astonishing collections of Qur'ans, *hadith* (sayings of the Prophet Muhammad), and *hadith* commentaries, as well as theological and legal works. Because of his active role in founding libraries and theological colleges, these books were disseminated to various parts of the Ottoman Empire, reinforcing the presence of the Hanafi legal rite and of the Ottoman brand of Sunni orthodoxy in general. At the same time, the schools he founded helped to ensure that boys and young men in far-flung Ottoman provinces would be trained in the official Ottoman version of Islam.

Like most chief harem eunuchs of the seventeenth and eighteenth centuries, Beshir Agha cultivated a link to Egypt, where he had been castrated following his enslavement in his native Ethiopia and where he was later exiled for approximately two years shortly before he was appointed chief eunuch. His connections to the provincial notables of Egypt helped to promote the Hanafi legal rite in a province in which this rite was not dominant. At the same time, these connections served as a channel of influence over the annual pilgrimage caravan sent from Cairo to Islam's Holy Cities, Mecca and Medina. (Islam was first revealed at Mecca, the Prophet Muhammad's birthplace and the site of the cubical stone structure known as the Ka'ba, to which all Muslims are enjoined to make a pilgrimage at least once in their lifetimes. Muhammad established the first Muslim community at Medina, to which he fled in 622 C.E. following years of harassment in Mecca; he is buried there, as well.)

The Holy Cities were a key preoccupation of the chief harem eunuch, who oversaw a massive network of pious endowments that benefited the populations of and Muslim pilgrims to Mecca and Medina. Beshir Agha's attachment to the Holy Cities went beyond supervision of the pious foundations, however. In the years immediately preceding his appointment as chief eunuch, he headed the corps of eunuchs who guarded the Prophet Muhammad's tomb in Medina. In "making the *hijra* to the Prophet" – an expression deriving from the Prophet's own migration, or *hijra*, to Medina in 622 – *before* his tenure as chief eunuch, he was unique among chief harem eunuchs. Devotion to the Prophet and to the Holy Cities characterized the chief harem eunuch, whose own quarters in the Ottoman imperial palace in Istanbul were decorated with representations of the Ka'ba in Mecca.

PLAN OF THE BOOK

This book begins by placing eunuchs within the broader context of elite slavery and membership in elite households, of which the Ottoman sultan's palace was the epitome. It then surveys the historical phenomenon of harem eunuchs up through the Ottoman period, devoting particular attention to Ottoman harem eunuchs and the office of chief eunuch. Following these preliminaries, the work focuses on the extraordinary career of Beshir Agha himself, drawing what conclusions it can about his little-known early life, then tracing his ascent to power. His close relationship with Gülnush Emetullah, favorite concubine of Sultan Mehmed IV (r. 1648–87) and mother of Sultan Ahmed III (r. 1703–30), receives particular attention, as does his astonishing ability to escape unscathed from the 1730 rebellion that resulted in Ahmed III's dethronement and the execution of his grand vizier. Central to the work are Beshir Agha's religious and intellectual pursuits; I explore his immense collection of books, as well as the mosques and other pious foundations he endowed empire-wide.

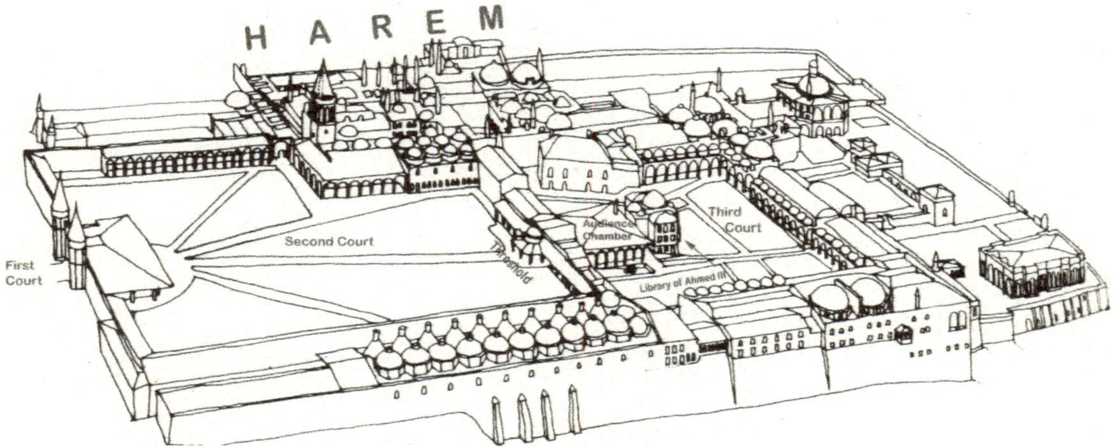

Figure 1: Plan of Topkapı Palace, from Robert Hillenbrand, *Islamic Architecture: Form, Function, and Meaning* (Edinburgh: Edinburgh University Press, 2000), p. 458. By permission of Robert Hillenbrand and Edinburgh University Press (www.eup.ed.ac.uk). Labels added.

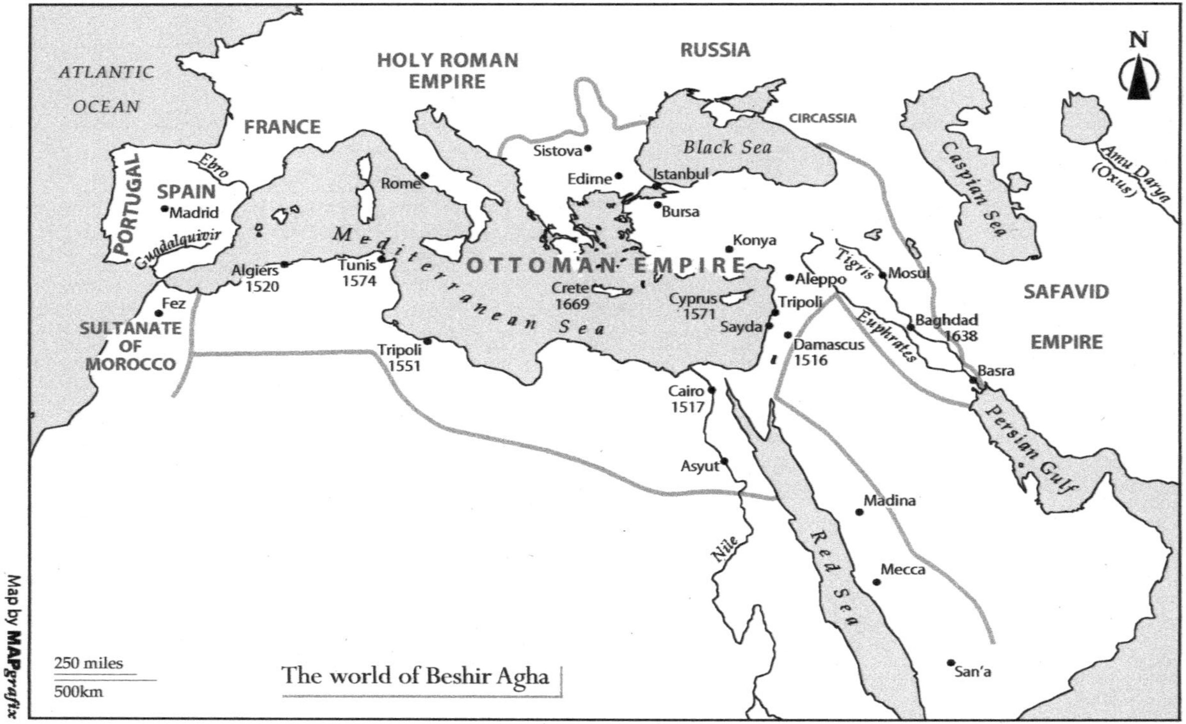

The Ottoman Empire c. 1700. (Dates are conquest dates.)

1

PRELIMINARIES: ELITE SLAVERY AND HOUSEHOLD MEMBERSHIP

ELITE SLAVERY IN ISLAMIC SOCIETIES

In most Islamic and non-Islamic societies in which they were employed, eunuchs – that is, castrated males – were slaves. However, they belonged to a special subcategory of elite slaves: high-status slaves, often attached to a ruler's court, who received all the privileges that accompanied their high status, including access to the finest education available and to lavish clothing, accoutrements, and accommodations. To understand the status that eunuchs enjoyed in Islamic societies in general and in the Ottoman Empire in particular, we must first become acquainted with this distinctive form of slavery of which eunuchhood was a part.

In many cases, men and women destined for elite slavery were removed from their families – and often from their native lands, as well – and enslaved for the express purpose of serving at the ruler's court, where, it was assumed, their lack of familial and community ties, as well as their dependence on the ruler for their privileges, would breed loyalty to the very ruler who had enslaved them. To the rulers who employed such slaves – from the Roman and Byzantine emperors to the emperors of the many Chinese dynasties to the Mughal emperors of India and the Ottomans – they seemed a better security risk than free subjects, who might acquire the same levels of education and political savvy but who came with the baggage with which attachment to a particular region and community inevitably encumbered them.

Islamic societies employed male elite slaves in two principal capacities: as military officers and as palace functionaries. In both cases, the slaves were taken into service at a young age – anywhere from the prepubescent years to young manhood – and converted to Islam. The distinction between these two categories was not infrequently blurred, however: a military commander might well wield influence and even occupy high office at the ruler's court, while a palace favorite might be preferred for high military command.

Mamluks

Military slaves, known as *mamluks*, from the Arabic word for "owned," were first employed systematically on a large scale by the Abbasid caliphs, who ruled much of the present-day Middle East from their capital at Baghdad from 762 through 1258. Beginning in the early decades of the ninth century, the Abbasids employed slave-soldiers from the Turkish principalities to their east both as military commanders and as rank-and-file soldiers. The proximity of these Central Asian Turkish peoples, combined with the semi-nomadic Turks' skills in horsemanship and archery, made them the prime source of mamluks until well after the Abbasid caliphate had been destroyed by the Mongols in the mid-thirteenth century. One ninth-century Abbasid caliph founded the city of Samarra, north of Baghdad on the Tigris River, as a sort of haven for himself and his Turkish mamluks. By the end of the ninth century, however, Turkic mamluk generals had conspired to dethrone and even to murder several Abbasid caliphs.

The Mamluk sultanate

Turkish mamluks from the Central Asian steppe remained a key component of the armies of various provincial regimes under nominal Abbasid rule until the Mongol invasions of the thirteenth century.

Toward the middle of that century, in the shadow of the Mongol threat, Turkish mamluks in Syria and Egypt displaced the dynasty that employed them, which had been founded by the legendary Crusader-routing Kurdish general Salah al-Din (known in Western Europe as Saladin), himself a client of the Turkish general whom the Abbasids recognized as governor of northern Iraq and Syria. The regime founded by these mamluks is known as the Mamluk sultanate. Mamluks under the sultanate were usually manumitted after completing their initial training; they could then ascend to the ranks of the military commanders and purchase their own mamluks, whom they, in turn, trained for high office. Although most Mamluk sultans attempted to groom their sons, if they had any, to succeed them, powerful mamluk military commanders continually usurped the throne, so that the sultanate was, for most of its existence, an oligarchy of manumitted elite slaves.

Toward the end of the thirteenth century, the Mamluk sultans began to supplement their supply of Central Asian Turkish mamluks with mamluks from the Caucasus Mountains, above all from the territory known as Circassia in the northeastern Black Sea region (today a southerly region of Russia). By the time the Ottoman Empire conquered the Mamluk sultanate in 1516–17, most sultans – and most of their mamluks – were Circassians. This was a key model of elite slavery for the Ottomans, particularly following their conquest of the Arab lands that had been under Mamluk sultanate rule.

The Ottoman devshirme

Yet the Ottomans, well before their conquest of the Mamluk domains, had perfected their own distinctive mode of elite slavery, accomplished by means of a recruitment system known in Turkish as *devshirme*, or "collection." Although it may have had antecedents in the recruitment of Greek and Armenian mamluks (or *ghulams*, as they were called) by the Turkish rulers of central Anatolia in the twelfth and thirteenth centuries (an offshoot of the Turkish regime to which Saladin's patron had been attached), the *devshirme* appears to date from the late fourteenth or early fifteenth century and to have been employed systematically following the Ottomans' conquest of the Balkans from the Byzantine Empire. By the terms of this system, recruiters would venture into the Ottomans' eastern European provinces roughly once each year and select a certain percentage of boys from the population of the Christian villages.

The distinctive feature of the *devshirme* was that the recruits were technically Ottoman subjects even though, according to the template for treatment of non-Muslim monotheists under Muslim rule in place since at least the eighth century, non-Muslim subjects of a Muslim ruler were supposed to be exempt from enslavement. Various Ottoman jurists and chroniclers justified this practice in Islamic legal terms by evoking the Muslim conqueror's right to one-fifth of all movable booty; by this logic, the Christian boys constituted the sultan's fifth. Notwithstanding this rationalization, convenience and expediency almost certainly underlay this practice, which was far less costly and perilous than procuring mamluks from outside the sultan's domains, often separated from those domains by hostile territory.

During the fifteenth and sixteenth centuries, *devshirme* recruits supplied the bulk of the Ottomans' palace pages, as well as their elite infantry corps, the fearsome Janissaries. In an initial selection, *devshirme* recruits who showed special intellectual aptitude were earmarked for palace service while the majority entered the Janissary corps. From the ranks of palace pages, the rare *devshirme* recruit might one day rise to become grand vizier, the Ottoman equivalent of a prime minister, or perhaps chief financial officer or governor of an important Ottoman province.

HOUSEHOLD POLITICS AND PATRON–CLIENT TIES

Elite slavery, including eunuchhood, cannot be properly understood outside the framework of the household. In this context, a household was a network of reciprocal ties of patronage and clientage, centering on the founder and/or head of the household. The ruler's court in most premodern societies was that society's preeminent household. Just as the ruler's household centered on his (or occasionally her) palace, so the households of lower-ranking officials centered on their own often palatial residences. The elite slave was, first and foremost, a member of such a household, bound to the household head not only by condition of servitude but also by the ties of obligation and loyalty that accompanied membership in the household.

The milieu inhabited by Ottoman eunuchs in many respects resembled a hierarchy of households. At the pinnacle of this hierarchy was the sultan's household, situated in the imperial palace in Istanbul, but below this were the households of various government ministers (viziers) and provincial governors, as well as the local notables – localized military officers, long-distance merchants, prominent Muslim scholar-officials – of the provinces. The chief harem eunuch attained his office by successfully negotiating the tangle of patron–client ties that characterized the sultan's household. Because of his connections to Egypt (discussed in chapters 2, 3, 5, and 9), furthermore, the chief eunuch, both before he attained that post and after he left it, formed lasting connections with the households of Egypt's grandees.

In the Ottoman palace, eunuchs were part of the population of members of the sultan's household, existing alongside and interacting with the pages recruited through the *devshirme*. Particularly during the sixteenth and early seventeenth centuries, they might serve as military commanders, as well. Eunuchs, however, did not usually come out of the *devshirme* but were recruited in a manner more closely resembling the purchase of mamluks. Before turning to Ottoman eunuchs specifically, however, we will find it useful to place the functions that eunuch elite slaves performed in historical perspective.

2

EUNUCHS IN HISTORICAL PERSPECTIVE

EUNUCHS IN ANTIQUITY

The use of eunuchs at the courts of rulers and in their armed forces dates back as far as the Assyrians, who ruled much of what are now Iraq and Syria from roughly 911 through 612 B.C.E. The famous stone friezes carved by the Assyrians and now on display in various museums world-wide show hunting scenes in which beardless courtiers, almost certainly eunuchs, appear alongside more hirsute kings and hunters. The courtiers called, in the singular, *saris* in Hebrew in the biblical book of Esther, which is supposed to have been composed under the ancient Persian, or Achaemenid, Empire (550–330 B.C.E.), are widely conceded to have been eunuchs. Indeed, Alexander the Great, who conquered the Achaemenid Empire in 330 B.C.E., is said to have become enamored of a young Persian eunuch taken from the court of the defeated Achaemenid emperor Darius III (r. 336–330 B.C.E.); this boy had apparently been taken captive by Darius' forces and castrated as a form of revenge against his father, who had run afoul of Darius. More conclusive among biblical references is the book of Isaiah's mention of eunuchs (again, *saris* in the singular) who will be accepted as members of the community of believers despite their mutilation.

Certainly, both of the enormous empires, the Byzantine, or Eastern Roman, and the Sasanian, or Persian, which ruled most of the region now known as the Middle East at the time of Islam's appearance in the early seventh century, C.E. used eunuchs on a large scale, both in their armies and at their courts. In addition to adhering to the widespread habit of employing eunuch military commanders and placing eunuch guards at the entrances to the imperial family's inner sanctum, the Byzantines introduced castrated male vocalists into their religious services as singers – in addition to more traditional non-eunuch singers – the better to replicate the heavenly choirs of angels. This custom prepared the way for the institution of *castrati*, castrated male sopranos, in European opera houses during the early modern era.

EUNUCHS IN MEDIEVAL ISLAMIC EMPIRES

So it was that the nascent Islamic polity, following the death of the Prophet Muhammad in 632 C.E., found itself expanding into the territory of two empires in which the employment of eunuchs was habitual. Accordingly, eunuchs shortly appeared in Islamic palaces and armies. The Umayyad caliphs, who ruled from 661 to 750, must certainly have employed eunuchs, although the surviving written and material record of their court practices is so meager as to offer no conclusive proof. For the Abbasids, who overthrew the Umayyads in 750 and established a new capital at Baghdad, we are on much firmer ground. A description of Abbasid Baghdad by a Syrian geographer in the ninth century describes chambers built into the enormous walls of the original round city, constructed in 762, to house African eunuch guards, pointing to importation of eastern African eunuchs very early in the Abbasid period. This is not terribly surprising given that non-eunuch eastern African slaves were an entrenched feature of Iraqi life, as evidenced by the massive and prolonged revolt (869–83) of the wretched African slaves who toiled in the salt marshes of southern Iraq. Annalistic chronicles of the Abbasid Empire also note Persian and Turkish eunuch military commanders who served the caliph beginning in the mid-ninth century, indicating an overlap between the functions of mamluks and those of eunuchs.

Regional powers in eastern Iran during the Abbasid period also employed eunuchs as both harem guardians and military commanders. Under the Great Seljuks, a semi-nomadic Turkish population who took over Iraq and Iran in the eleventh century, eunuchs appear to have served variously as harem guardians, tutors to crown princes, and pleasure companions to the rulers; it is not difficult to see how the same eunuch could have fulfilled all three functions. Some of the Seljuks' eunuchs are called "black" in Seljuk chronicles, although what this implies about their provenance is impossible to determine with certainty. Given the heavy use of eastern African slaves under the Abbasids, we might easily conclude that the Seljuks, coming into Abbasid territory, exploited the same African pool of manpower. Yet, in view of the commercial links that Iran and Iraq enjoyed with India, these "blacks" might also have included Indian slaves.

In the Muslim West, the Abbasids' arch-enemies, the Ismaili Shi'ite caliphs of the Fatimid dynasty, who ripped North Africa, Egypt, Syria, and the western Arabian peninsula from Abbasid control during the tenth century, employed slaves from the Sudan as mamluks and eunuchs alike. The Fatimids also employed eunuchs from a population known as *Saqaliba*, a label apparently applied to a variety of Slavic and other eastern European peoples. In one famous Mediterranean naval engagement, the commanders of both the Fatimid and the Byzantine fleet were eunuchs. In Spain, various parts of which were under Muslim rule between 711 and 1492 C.E., most eunuchs, whether military commanders or harem guardians, were likewise *Saqaliba*. In the post-Fatimid period, the Seljuk offshoot which ruled eastern and central Anatolia from roughly 1077 to 1307 employed Greek and Armenian eunuchs, as did the principalities of western Anatolia which preceded and/or were contemporaneous with the early Ottomans in the same region. In Anatolia, one assumes, the Byzantine prototype for court eunuchs was especially influential.

EUNUCHS UNDER THE MAMLUK SULTANATE

Arguably, however, the Muslim polity from which the Ottoman Empire drew most inspiration in its employment of eunuchs was the

Mamluk sultanate, which ruled Egypt, Syria, the western Arabian peninsula, and southeastern Anatolia from 1250 until its conquest by the Ottomans in 1516–17. The Mamluk sultanate is distinctive among Islamic – and all other – polities in that it was ruled by elite slaves, known as *mamluks* (from the Arabic word for "owned"), who were purchased from the steppe north of the Black Sea or from the Caucasus Mountains. In a variation of earlier polities' use of eunuchs as military commanders, the Mamluks entrusted eunuchs with supervising the education, both military and otherwise, of the raw mamluk recruits newly arrived in Cairo. As David Ayalon has noted, part of the motive for this practice must have been to prevent sexual abuse of the newcomers by older mamluks in the barracks.

Tomb eunuchs

Of greater significance, at least so far as later Ottoman tradition was concerned, was the Mamluks' innovation in assigning eunuchs to guard the tombs of sultans in Cairo, and ultimately appointing a corps of eunuchs to guard the tomb of the Prophet Muhammad in Medina. (The Turkic rulers of southern Iraq in roughly the same period, it is worth noting, employed eunuch guardians at the tomb of Ali, the Prophet Muhammad's son-in-law, in Najaf.) Historian Shaun Marmon has illuminated the circumstances surrounding the apparent twelfth-century origins of the practice of assigning eunuchs to the Prophet's tomb, commonly attributed to the great Crusader-fighter Saladin and/or his patron, the autonomous governor of northern Iraq and Syria mentioned in chapter 1.

The Mamluks' reinforcement of this practice when they displaced Saladin's dynasty in the mid-thirteenth century coincided with a concerted Mamluk attempt to shore up Sunni Islam in Medina. For Medina, both under Fatimid rule and under the rule of the Fatimids' Sunni successors, had become a stronghold of Muslim scholar-officials from the minority Zaydi and Ismaili subsects of Shi'ite Islam, to be discussed in connection with the tomb eunuchs in chapter 6. The Mamluks introduced a "row of eunuchs" who stood in front of the pulpit of the Prophet's mosque, where the Mamluk-appointed Sunni prayer leader presided over the public noontime prayer each Friday, in order to intimidate Shi'ite worshipers who might be tempted to create a disturbance. Likewise, a corps of eunuchs stood guard at the Prophet's tomb to limit access by the population of Medina at large to this sacred site. The institution of the tomb eunuchs continued until the conquest of Medina by the Saudis in the 1920s. As the puritanical brand of Sunni Islam practiced by the Saudis would not countenance the eunuch guard, those eunuchs remaining in Medina at the time of the conquest were pensioned off by the Saudi government.

EUNUCHS UNDER THE OTTOMANS

Ottoman use of eunuchs in the imperial palace dates at least to the reign of Sultan Murad II (r. 1421–51). However, Greek slaves are attested at the court of the second Ottoman sultan, Orhan (r. 1326–62), who ruled first from Iznik (the Byzantine Nicaea) in western Anatolia, taken from the Byzantines in 1326, then from Bursa (Byzantine Prusa), southwest of Iznik, after capturing it from the Byzantines in 1331; it is certainly conceivable that some of these slaves were eunuchs. If so, they were almost certainly eunuchs of the harem sort, responsible for guarding the private quarters of the sultan, his wives and concubines, and other members of the imperial family. Eunuch warriors, on the other hand, would not have been possible before the Ottomans undertook the systematic use of elite slaves in their armies in the fifteenth century.

The empire's so-called "golden age" under Sultan Süleyman I (r. 1520–66) featured a number of famous eunuch commanders, notably Süleyman Pasha, the admiral who conquered Yemen in 1538. (Officials holding the rank of minister to the Ottoman court or governor of a major Ottoman province received the title *pasha*, derived from the Persian for "for the king.") Some of these eunuch commanders were originally Orthodox Christians living in Anatolia or the Balkans; others, like Süleyman Pasha, who also served as grand vizier from 1541–53, were Hungarian. In the latter half of the century, eunuchs from the Caucasus, above all Georgia, become more noticeable.

Eunuchs in the Ottoman palace

Eunuchs appear to have formed part of the personnel of the Ottoman palace in Istanbul, known as Topkapı, or "cannon gate," virtually from its construction under Sultan Mehmed II ("the Conqueror") following his 1453 conquest of Constantinople from the Byzantines. Initially, these were largely white eunuchs from the Balkans, Hungary, and the Caucasus who guarded the threshold separating the palace's Second Court, where soldiers, ambassadors, and other outside visitors might gather, from the Third Court, forbidden to all but the sultan's family and personal servants; just past this threshold stood the sultan's audience chamber. This "male harem" formed a counterpart to the "female harem," inhabited by the sultan's mother, sisters, wives, and concubines, which until the reign of Süleyman I was located in the "Old Palace," which Mehmed the Conqueror had built shortly after his conquest of the city on the site of the former Forum of Theodosius, now the site of Istanbul University. At the behest of Süleyman's influential wife, the female harem was removed to Topkapı, where it would ultimately occupy a large complex of buildings on the western side of the Third Court. The presence of the female harem within the Topkapı Palace compound provided an opportunity for the sultan's wives and concubines, as well as other women of the imperial family, to exert an unprecedented degree of influence not only on palace affairs but on imperial policy. As for the eunuchs, they henceforth guarded not only the threshold of the Third Court but the entrance to the female harem, as well.

The harem eunuchs were initially, by all accounts, a mixed group of white and African eunuchs. The conquest of the Mamluk sultanate by Süleyman's father, Selim I (r. 1512–20), had given the Ottomans easy access to the trade in African slaves through the Sudan to Cairo. Under Süleyman, furthermore, the region known as Abyssinia, encompassing the coastal regions of present-day Ethiopia and a large swatch of present-day Sudan, came within the Ottoman orbit. In consequence, large numbers of Abyssinian and other eastern African eunuchs began to flow into the Ottoman palace and the households of Ottoman provincial governors and grandees. Abyssinians would come to be the most highly valued eunuchs among the Ottomans. Indeed, the Ottoman term for Abyssinians – singular, Habeshi – distinguished them from other sub-Saharan Africans, known collectively as Zanj. The eunuchs who guarded the threshold in front of the sultan's audience chamber at the entrance to the palace's Third Court, known in Arabic and Ottoman Turkish as the "Gate of Felicity," remained white eunuchs from Europe or the Caucasus.

The population of Topkapı Palace reached its highest numbers during the reign of Sultan Murad III (r. 1574–95), when the number of eunuchs correspondingly peaked at roughly 1,000 to 1,200. Some 600 to 800 of these were harem eunuchs under the supervision of the chief harem eunuch, an officer first appointed by Murad III whose official title was "Guardian of the Abode of Felicity," referring to the harem. Racial and color distinctions between the eunuchs of the Abode of Felicity and those of the Gate of Felicity (that is, the threshold in front of the sultan's audience chamber) sharpened during these years; by 1592, the post of chief harem eunuch was dominated by eastern Africans, that of chief threshold eunuch by white eunuchs from the Caucasus and Eastern Europe.

Although still inadequately understood, this racial polarization must certainly have been linked to the supervision of a set of important imperial pious endowments to the Holy Cities of Mecca and Medina. Revenues from land and properties all over the empire were endowed to these foundations, which provided food, water, and other amenities to the poor of Mecca and Medina, as well as to Muslim pilgrims to these two cities. The foundations included several royal endowments founded under the Mamluk sultanate, as well as more recent Ottoman foundations. Süleyman's wife had herself founded one of the largest endowments. Her endowment deed stipulated that her foundation would be supervised by the chief threshold eunuch, but this was the last time this official would receive control of a major imperial pious foundation. Shortly thereafter, in fact, the chief harem eunuch came to supervise all other Holy Cities foundations collectively. Initially, the chief threshold eunuch could likewise function as overall supervisor of the endowments, but by 1592, the chief harem eunuch had gained exclusive right to this office. This meant that the chief harem eunuch had an intimate connection with the Holy Cities, even while in office in Istanbul. When, in the late seventeenth century, it became routine for former chief harem eunuchs to be appointed chiefs of the eunuchs who guarded the Prophet's tomb in Medina, the link became closer still.

Why Africans?

Regarding the preference for Africans to guard the women's harem, the British diplomat Sir Paul Rycaut, whose *Present State of the Ottoman Empire* provides an invaluable window onto the workings of the palace in the mid-seventeenth century, claims that harem women find Africans physically repellent:

> ... it not seeming a sufficient remedy by wholly dismembering them, to take the Women off from their inclinations to them, as retaining some relation still to the Masculine Sex, but to create an abhorrency in them, they are not only castrated but black, chosen with the worst features that are to be found among the most hard-favoured of that African race.
>
> (Rycaut 1668, p. 37)

Naturally, such a statement is far more revealing of Rycaut's own racial attitudes than it is of the realities of the harem, however valuable his work may otherwise be.

A more plausible explanation may have to do with the unprecedented numbers of eunuchs, both black and white, entering the palace toward the end of the sixteenth century. Growing numbers of young men from the same general region of eastern Africa no doubt fostered ethno-regional solidarity, as did the parallel phenomenon of growing numbers of young men from Hungary or, later, from Circassia and Georgia. With increasing numbers came gradual polarization of the two groups of eunuchs. Why the East Africans concentrated in the female harem while the Hungarians, and later Caucasians, concentrated in the male harem is less clear. The fact that the male harem, which predated the female harem, had from its inception been guarded by white eunuchs may argue for a continuation of the custom through sheer inertia. The female harem was introduced to Topkapı Palace shortly before the influx of Abyssinian eunuchs began; thus, it may have offered them a space that the male harem did not.

Apart from these spatial and chronological concerns, however, employing East Africans to guard female harems appears to have been a venerable practice in the Middle East well before the rise of the Ottoman Empire. African eunuchs guard the emperor's harem in the *1001 Nights*, a collection of stories dealing primarily with ninth-century Baghdad. Given that most harem inmates, in ninth-century Baghdad as in sixteenth-century Istanbul, were white, hailing variously from Central Asia, the Caucasus, and, in the case of the Ottoman harem, the Balkans, employing African eunuchs to guard them may have made sexual contact between the harem women and their guardians seem relatively unlikely. The color barrier would have added to the estrangement of the guardians from those they guarded created by the vast difference in geographical and cultural provenance. Had the harem guards come from the same regions and cultural backgrounds as the harem women, on the other hand, such contact would have been far more likely to occur. Repellent as Rycaut's racial attitudes may seem to us today, he may have a legitimate point about the sheer "otherness" of African eunuchs in the eyes of women from the Caucasus and Balkans.

The polarization of the two populations of eunuchs may seem even more comprehensible if we consider the serious effects of ethno-regional solidarity on Ottoman military and administrative personnel during the seventeenth century, which witnessed mounting antagonism between "westerners" from the Balkans and western Anatolia, on the one hand, and "easterners" from the Caucasus, on the other. Where palace eunuchs were concerned, the difference in skin color between the African population and populations hailing from eastern Europe or the Caucasus would only have exacerbated the estrangement resulting from ethno-regional differences. Yet even an explanation based on ethno-regional solidarity almost certainly fails fully to explain this division of labor between African and non-African eunuchs at the end of the sixteenth century; geography and expediency may indeed have played a larger role than we suspect. At the least, however, we must discard the notion that the division is entirely understandable in terms of modern-day racial attitudes.

Deposition and exile to Egypt

It was highly unusual for a chief harem eunuch to hold that office until his death. Beshir Agha was one of the very few chief eunuchs in Ottoman history to do so. Typically, the chief harem eunuch ran afoul of a new sultan or a new grand vizier, or of the sultan's mother or one of the sultan's concubines or an official in her entourage, and was peacefully deposed from office. This sort of dismissal was by the late sixteenth century a routine part of the political careers of a wide range of Ottoman officials. A deposed chief eunuch, like other deposed officials, might expect to be exiled from the Ottoman capital; this measure was taken not to ruin the official in question but to remove him from the center of political power.

Beginning in the mid-seventeenth century, deposed chief harem eunuchs, as well as harem eunuchs dismissed from lower ranks, were routinely exiled to Cairo for reasons that remain unclear. The fact that African harem eunuchs were initially sold in Egypt before arriving at the imperial palace in Istanbul, as will be noted in the following chapter, doubtless had something to do with the practice, as did Egypt's sheer distance from the imperial capital. An exiled chief harem eunuch could expect to live out his life in Cairo, although beginning in the late seventeenth century, a stint as chief of the eunuchs who guarded the Prophet Muhammad's tomb in Medina might interrupt the Egyptian sojourn. As a result, a community of exiled eunuchs took shape in Egypt and had a decisive impact on that province's political culture and economy. Beshir Agha was unusual in that his own Egyptian exile, like his tenure as chief of the eunuchs guarding the Prophet's tomb, occurred *before* he was appointed chief harem eunuch.

3

BESHIR AGHA'S ORIGINS

OTTOMAN ABYSSINIA

Beshir Agha must have been born around 1655 in Abyssinia (Habesh in Ottoman Turkish), which in an Ottoman context meant the territory conquered by Ottoman forces under the Ottoman governor of Yemen in the 1550s. At its greatest extent in the late sixteenth century, the province of Abyssinia extended from the southern border of Egypt all the way to the Horn of Africa, encompassing most of present-day Sudan, Djibouti on the Horn of Africa, and coastal Ethiopia. Since its conquest, this region had been administered by an Ottoman governor technically equivalent in rank to the governor of any major Ottoman province, such as Egypt, Damascus, or Rumeli (that is, southeastern Europe collectively). During the seventeenth century, the governor of Abyssinia was routinely chosen from among the subprovincial governors of Egypt; at the beginning of the eighteenth century, the governorship of Abyssinia was combined with the post of military governor of Mecca. This governor almost certainly played some part in the acquisition of Abyssinian young men, young women, boys, and girls for the slave trade through Sudan to Egypt.

From the standpoint of Islamic law, the procurement of Abyssinian slaves posed challenges similar to those presented by the *devshirme* since most of Abyssinia's population remained Christian: as noted in chapter 1, non-Muslim monotheists – predominantly Christians and Jews – under Muslim rule were legally exempt from enslavement. Christianity had taken root in Egypt and the Horn of Africa in the third and fourth centuries C.E., and most Abyssinians adhered to the form of the religion practiced in Egypt. Indeed, until the 1950s, when the legendary Ethiopian emperor Haile Salassie declared it independent, Ethiopia's church remained subordinate to the Coptic church in Egypt; the Coptic Pope sent a bishop to Ethiopia from Alexandria. Notwithstanding, the rulers of Ethiopia had a venerable practice of employing eunuchs from among their own countrymen at their court, as witness the passage in the New Testament regarding "an Ethiopian, a eunuch, a minister of Candace the queen of the Ethiopians, in charge of all her treasure" (Acts 8: 27–8). Such time-honored usages, combined with the tradition of African eunuchs in the palace harems of Islamic empires, may have made it easier to circumvent the objections of Islamic law.

ENSLAVEMENT AND CASTRATION

Abyssinians were especially highly prized in the trans-Saharan slave trade; higher prices were paid for Abyssinian eunuchs than for eunuchs of any other provenance, whether African or (literally) Caucasian. Like other young Abyssinians selected for this trade, the young Beshir (whose original Abyssinian name, like those of other African slaves, is unknown) would have been transported in frequently brutal conditions in one of the two major slave caravans that traversed the deserts of Sudan each year: one from the city of Sennar in what is now southeastern Sudan, one from the Darfur region in what is now western Sudan. (A third caravan arrived occasionally from northwestern Africa.) During the late sixteenth and the seventeenth centuries, the caravan route from Sennar to Cairo would have lain entirely within Ottoman territory. From Sennar, several small caravans set out at various times of year, coming together at Egypt's southern frontier to form one larger caravan for the trip to Cairo. The Sennar caravan was much smaller than the Darfur caravan, bringing in only a few hundred slaves a year, most of them female. By contrast, the Darfur caravan at the end of the eighteenth century was bringing some five to six thousand slaves to Egypt annually.

Some slaves were also transported by boat from one of several ports on the Red Sea coast of Africa to Suez and various ports in Arabia and Yemen.

Abyssinian youths destined to become eunuchs were castrated in villages in Upper Egypt inhabited by Coptic Christians; the villages just south of Asyut were key centers. Because castration was against Islamic law, the operation usually took place at the peripheries of Ottoman territory and was typically performed by Christian physicians: near the Caucasus, Armenian physicians, near the Sudan, Coptic physicians. Even so, there are accounts of castrations performed within Topkapı Palace itself.

African eunuchs typically underwent so-called "radical" castration, in which both the testicles and the penis were removed, whereas in the case of eunuchs from Europe and the Caucasus, only the testicles were removed. The reasons for this difference remain unclear. Historic castration practice in the Nile river valley surely played a part; African eunuchs employed by the Fatimid caliphs and the Mamluk sultans, who ruled Egypt in the centuries before the Ottoman conquest, were similarly radically castrated, to the best of our knowledge. In addition, since sub-Saharan Africa has a large pool of endemic diseases, relative to mountainous northerly regions such as southeastern Europe and the Caucasus, natural immunity would have been greater among African youths than among youths from the Balkans or the Caucasus. They would thus have had a higher chance of surviving post-castration infections, all other things being equal, thus perhaps making the radical operation appear less risky in their case and providing no pretext for discontinuing the practice.

According to the account of John Lewis Burckhardt, who visited Upper Egypt and Nubia in the early nineteenth century, though he did not witness the operation in person, the young man was held down on top of a table while his genitalia were tied off with "soap-coated silken cords" (Burckhardt 1831, p. 329). They were then swiftly cut off with a razor. Following surgery, a wooden or tin tube was inserted into the new eunuch's urethra, the wound was cauterized with ash and hot sand, then slightly later with boiling oil, and the patient underwent what must often have been an agonizing three-day waiting period during which he was not allowed to urinate. At the end of this period, the wound was uncovered, and if no infection were observed and the new eunuch were able to urinate without obstruction, the operation was pronounced a success. The wound was then dressed with a special Coptic plaster, the ingredients of which, Burckhardt claims, were a closely guarded secret, for forty more days, until it had scarred. Both Burckhardt and Sir Richard Francis Burton claim that mortality from the operation was remarkably low; they are joined in this opinion by the French physician Louis Franck, who lived in Egypt at the end of the eighteenth century. Indeed, Burckhardt claims that of sixty boys castrated near the Upper Egyptian city of Asyut in the autumn of 1813, only two died, despite what might seem a high risk of death from blood loss or post-surgical infection.

The case of the Hungarian eunuch Gazanfer Agha, however, suggests that mortality may occasionally have been higher. Gazanfer and his brother, Hungarian Christians taken into palace service, became close confidants of the future sultan Selim II (r. 1566–74). When Selim took the throne, they knew that they would have to become eunuchs if they were to retain their intimacy with him; apart from blood relatives, no other type of male would be allowed such close contact. They therefore voluntarily underwent castration. Of the two, however, only Gazanfer survived the operation. Being from a relatively northerly European clime, of course, the two presumably had lower natural immunity than their African counterparts; the fact that they were adults when they underwent the surgery may also have increased the risk. Having survived, in any case, Gazanfer went on to become chief of the guardians of the threshold in front of the sultan's audience chamber, and one of the more influential figures in the late sixteenth-century Ottoman Empire.

Chinese eunuchs are known to have preserved their severed genitalia in special lacquered boxes which were buried with them on their deaths. This custom is not generally known among Ottoman eunuchs, although an early eighteenth-century treatise denouncing African eunuchs claims that one African eunuch employed at Topkapı Palace possessed such a box.

POST-CASTRATION CONDITIONS

Even if he survived, the new eunuch could expect to suffer lifelong discomfort and even pain as a result of the castration. Urinary-tract infections were a common complaint; incontinence often followed as the eunuch aged. Chinese folk sayings include the simile "as stinky as a eunuch," presumably because of the pervasive odor of urine that clung to many eunuchs. European visitors to Istanbul noted that the Topkapı Palace eunuchs placed silver quills in the folds of their turbans; they would use these as catheters when they urinated. The historian Shaun Marmon came across a eunuch under the Mamluk sultanate who "leaked" urine and had to wear a special receptacle, rather like a boot, to catch it.

If the eunuch were castrated before puberty, as most eunuchs in court service were, he would probably suffer from osteoporosis in later life, since his bones would not have undergone the development and strengthening typically brought on by surging testosterone levels at puberty. On the other hand, his arms and legs would grow disproportionately long relative to his torso; medical X-rays of late Ottoman eunuchs taken in the early twentieth century show fingers reaching nearly to the eunuchs' knees. As a result of hormonal deficiencies, eunuchs were either prone to obesity or, on the other hand, remained underweight and therefore appeared unusually slender and delicate. (Beshir was apparently a rather stout man.) For the same reason, their skin would wrinkle prematurely, creating an odd contrast to their beardless faces; meanwhile, their faces were often disproportionately large. The eunuch's voice never broke, remaining relatively high-pitched throughout his life. By the time he reached old age – and a eunuch who survived the castration operation had a good chance of living into his eighties or even nineties – his voice could resemble what Chinese sources describe as that of a shrieking old woman. Sir Richard Francis Burton claims, however, that the eunuch's hoarse voice inspired awe and respect, thus contributing to an authoritative aura. (He further claims that, owing to emasculation, a eunuch sat a horse well and was thus at an advantage over non-eunuchs in certain military skills – a rather implausible rationalization, it would seem, for the heavy use of eunuchs as military commanders under the Ottomans and earlier regimes.)

Supposedly "scientific" studies of the early twentieth century, which had a disproportionate influence on contemporary and slightly later writing on Ottoman eunuchs, attributed all manner of tastes and predilections to the eunuch's physical state: preference for the color red, affinity for cats and small birds, love of music, a taste for sweetmeats, and so on. These are obviously the observed tastes of a narrow sample of late Ottoman eunuchs and have no basis in physiology. (Indeed, it is hardly surprising that eunuchs employed by the Ottoman court would express a preference for red, the Ottoman dynastic color.)

Much has been written on whether eunuchs, even radically castrated ones, retained any sexual sensation or desire. The consensus of European observers, in any case, seems to have been that they remained receptive to sexual stimulation for at least a brief period after castration. The degree of stimulation and the length of this period varied according to the age at which the eunuch was castrated. Young boys who were several years away from puberty when castrated were unlikely to become susceptible to sexual impulses, whereas a youth castrated just after the onset of puberty would be most vulnerable. Numerous European writers have pointed out that a eunuch who retained his penis was still capable of sexual intercourse; such writers have not infrequently claimed that harem women habitually slaked their sexual desires with the aid of such eunuchs, and that the danger of such depravity lay behind the preference for radical castration of harem eunuchs under the Ottomans. The reality of the Topkapı Palace harem, however, in which the sultan's mother and her entourage of female servants maintained fairly rigid control over the sexuality of younger harem inmates, would probably have discouraged such scenarios; in parallel fashion, the chief eunuch and other senior eunuchs would have controlled the sexuality of younger harem eunuchs. This means, of course, that there was undeniable sexuality that needed to be controlled, and it is only to be expected that young women, many of them virgins, in such a tightly supervised environment would have experienced some degree of frustration.

There was almost certainly the very occasional tryst between harem girl and eunuch harem guardian. In general, however, there is no reason to doubt that eunuchs in the Ottoman harem served the same purpose as eunuchs in Mamluk barracks: that is, to act as a check on, rather than an enabler of, unbridled sexuality.

SALE IN CAIRO

Having come through the ordeal of castration, Beshir and the other surviving eunuchs would have been transported down the Nile to Cairo, where they were sold on the slave market. Only the Ottoman governor of Egypt and the wealthiest of Egypt's provincial grandees could afford to buy Abyssinian eunuchs, however. Far more numerous and far less expensive were sub-Saharan slave girls who were destined to live out their lives as household servants. If such a girl were "lucky," she might give birth to her master's son, whereupon the baby would receive the status of a free Muslim, and his mother would acquire this status on her master's death. Costly eunuchs such as Beshir, however, were purchased only by the heads of great military-administrative households. Numerous Abyssinian eunuchs were purchased by the Ottoman governor of Egypt, who not infrequently presented eunuchs to the sultan as gifts. Thus, many of the African eunuchs who guarded the imperial harem in Topkapı Palace may have spent time earlier in their lives in the household of the governor of Egypt, where they presumably learned the rudiments of Ottoman court protocol while acquiring a basic Islamic education.

THE POLITICAL CULTURE OF OTTOMAN EGYPT

Egypt was the Ottoman Empire's largest province and the one which generated the largest tax revenues for the imperial coffers. The conquest of this enormous, strategically located territory from the Mamluk sultanate in the early sixteenth century allowed the Ottomans to control the greater Red Sea region and gave them a jumping-off point for the annexation of the Sudan and Ethiopia. At the same time, a sizeable military and administrative infrastructure was necessary to run the province. In addition to the Ottoman governor and a supreme judge, both appointed from Istanbul, a chief financial officer and a pilgrimage commander were chosen from among the local or localized governors of Egypt's thirteen subprovinces, each of whom held the rank of *bey*. Seven regiments of Ottoman soldiery, each with its peculiar hierarchy of officers, maintained the peace in the provincial capital, Cairo, and the subprovinces, while ostensibly remaining ready to fight the empire's external enemies.

In the course of the sixteenth century, military and administrative personnel appear to have poured into Egypt from the imperial capital and from the Ottoman European provinces. By the end of the century, however, the governor of Egypt and the various subprovincial governors, as well as the higher officers of the seven regiments, were already acquiring military slaves from the Mamluk sultanate's old pool of manpower, namely, the Caucasus region and above all Circassia (now a part of Russia, northwest of the republic of Georgia). At the same time, Bedouin tribesmen and even Arabophone townsmen were finding their way into Egypt's military forces. This rather perplexing regional and ethnic mix may have underlain the abrupt appearance in the early seventeenth century of two implacably opposed political and military factions, known as the Faqaris and the Qasimis. Initially, the Faqaris seem to have represented Balkan and Anatolian elements, the Qasimis (literal) Caucasian elements, although later in the seventeenth century the Qasimis would come to include a sizeable Bosnian contingent, as well. From roughly 1640 through 1730, the Faqaris and Qasimis divided virtually all of Egyptian society – from regimental officers and subprovincial governors to peasants, Bedouin tribes, and rank-and-file soldiers – in two, in the manner of implacably opposed factions such as the Guelphs and Ghibellines of medieval northern Italy or the Hatfields and McCoys of the antebellum United States. Any eunuch attempting to negotiate Egyptian society would have confronted the factional divide and would almost certainly have joined or patronized one faction or the other.

Even these two factions, however, consisted of multiple households, and it was through household affiliation that a eunuch transported to Egypt would have gained entry into factional politics. Even if Beshir had entered the Ottoman governor's household, he would certainly have found that the governor favored one faction over the other in appointments and alliances. What little we are able to glean about Beshir's sojourn in Egypt immediately after his enslavement suggests that he himself was in a position to support the Faqari faction.

ISMAIL BEY

In point of fact, Beshir's initial owner may have been not the Ottoman governor of Egypt but another provincial grandee, if one eighteenth-century chronicle is to be believed. This chronicle, compiled in a very colloquial Arabic sometime around 1755, contains an intriguing vignette in which officials of the imperial governing council in Istanbul recommend their favorites for key posts in Egypt in 1733. The chief harem eunuch, who at the time would have been Beshir Agha, is supposed to have said, "And for chief financial officer, the son of my master (*sayyidi*) Ismail Bey" (al-Damurdashi *c.*1755, p. 407). This remark refers to Mehmed Bey the son of Ismail Bey, who indeed assumed the post of chief financial officer of Egypt. What is so intriguing, however, is that Beshir Agha ostensibly refers to Mehmed Bey's father, Ismail Bey, as "my master."

This Ismail Bey had himself held the post of chief financial officer of Egypt for many years at the end of the seventeenth century and the beginning of the eighteenth. He was the son-in-law of the commander of one of Egypt's seven regiments of Ottoman soldiery. Together with another regimental commander, Ismail Bey and his father-in-law virtually ran Egypt during these decades.

It is at least conceivable that Ismail Bey acquired the young Beshir in Egypt *c.*1667, although Ismail would himself have been quite a young man at the time. More generally, however, an interest in acquiring African eunuchs who might ultimately be presented to the imperial palace would have been natural to Egypt's grandees, and to these three grandees above all. Ismail Bey's father-in-law held the tax farms of a cluster of villages in Upper Egypt that were endowed to the imperial pious foundations for the Holy Cities of Mecca and Medina, which were under the chief harem eunuch's supervision. Connections to the chief harem eunuch meant a better chance of acquiring the tax farms of endowed villages; hence the attraction of presenting a eunuch protégé to the imperial harem in the hope that he might one day become chief eunuch.

Ismail Bey and his father-in-law were also anchors of the Faqari faction during the late seventeenth and early eighteenth centuries. Thus, if Beshir had belonged to Ismail's household early in his career as a eunuch, he would have been a *de facto* member of the Faqari faction through his affiliation to Ismail Bey. This may in part explain his tendency, much later in life, to favor the Faqaris where matters Egyptian were concerned.

The name Beshir and the title agha

If Ismail Bey really were Beshir's first master, then it is possible that he named the young eunuch Beshir. This was not a "typical" Ottoman eunuch name. These tended to be names of flowering plants or precious stones; hence Sünbül ("Hyacinth") Agha, Reyhan ("Sweet Basil") Agha, Merjan ("Coral") Agha. There were also numerous harem eunuchs who bore typical Muslim male names, such as Mehmed, Ahmed, and Mustafa. "Beshir" (Arabic, *bashīr*), in contrast, refers to a bearer of glad tidings and hence is often associated with various Christian themes, such as the Annunciation. As a eunuch name, it may conceivably have represented a sort of concession to the former Christian faith of Abyssinian eunuchs. Curiously, however, the name seems to have been restricted to African eunuchs, even though eunuchs from Hungary or Georgia were also, for the most part, Christians before enslavement.

Even before our Beshir Agha became one of the wealthiest, most powerful, and longest-lived chief harem eunuchs in Ottoman history, the name Beshir occurred with a fair degree of frequency among Ottoman harem eunuchs – although our Beshir was the first of that name to ascend to the post of chief eunuch. Following his tenure, however, the frequency of the name among chief harem eunuchs is striking. Indeed, the prefix "el-Hajj," referring to someone who has made the pilgrimage to Mecca – which Beshir apparently performed at some point before becoming chief eunuch – is often attached to our Beshir's name to distinguish him from later chief eunuchs named Beshir.

Agha, meanwhile, is a flexible title often used during the Ottoman era to designate the highest-ranking officer or officers in a particular military regiment. At the same time, the eunuchs of the Ottoman imperial palace carried the title *agha*, regardless of whether they served the harem or the threshold in front of the sultan's audience chamber and regardless of what rank they held in the eunuch hierarchy. The title seems also to have carried over to eunuchs serving outside the imperial palace, in the Ottoman provinces or at the tomb of the Prophet Muhammad in Medina. Thus, it is safe to assume that Beshir acquired the title *agha* almost as soon as he was enslaved. Ultimately, despite the continued use of the title to designate non-eunuch military commanders, *agha* became virtually synonymous with "eunuch" in an Ottoman context.

4

EARLY YEARS IN THE PALACE

The capsule biography of Beshir Agha provided by the *Sicill-i Osmani*, a sort of late nineteenth-century historical Ottoman "Who's Who," notes that Beshir was the protégé of the chief eunuch Yapraksız Ali Agha, who held that office from 1694 to 1700. (The connotations of the sobriquet Yapraksız, literally "leafless," are unclear.) Yapraksız Ali had served as tutor to the palace pages during the 1680s but, like many Ottoman officials, eunuch or otherwise, ran afoul of one higher-up or another and was exiled to Cairo from Istanbul. This sort of exile was, by the late seventeenth century, a routine part of most palace careers; the exiled official was not ruined for life but simply removed from the imperial capital to a provincial locale in which, ideally, he could not wield influence or build up any sort of power base. Such an official often received a stipend during his period of exile. He stood a fairly good chance of being summoned back to palace service after several years had passed. Beginning in the mid-seventeenth century, as noted in chapter 2, harem eunuchs were routinely exiled to Cairo, which, as a consequence, acquired a sizeable population of exiled palace eunuchs. Yapraksız Ali, following the pattern just described, was pardoned in 1694 and returned to the palace as chief eunuch. It is possible that he took Beshir back to Istanbul with him and promoted his career in the palace.

By 1694, Beshir was in his late thirties. We do not know how he had been employed until then. He would probably have been manumitted by Ismail Bey, the influential chief financial officer mentioned in the previous chapter, well before he reached this age, since this was the customary practice of grandees who owned elite slaves in Ottoman Egypt. He could well have come to Istanbul much earlier than 1694. In that case, any education in court protocol and Islamic doctrine that he might have received in the household of Ismail Bey in Cairo would have been augmented many times over.

Typically, eunuchs recently arrived at Topkapı Palace from Africa received a solid Islamic education within the harem compound, modeled on the palace pages' education, which occurred in special schoolrooms on the eastern side of the palace's Third Court, across the courtyard from the harem. In the harem school, the youngest eunuchs were strictly supervised by older eunuchs – lending credence to the hypothesis, noted in chapter 3, that the eunuchs' sexuality, like that of the harem women, was tightly controlled by means of a hierarchy of age. Once this basic training was completed, at about age 11, the young eunuch entered the service of the sultan's mother, under the ultimate supervision of the chief harem eunuch himself. At this stage, he received a clothing allowance, as well as a daily cash allowance. This may have allowed him to purchase the various trinkets and gadgets occasionally purveyed to the harem by western European merchants, with whom the chief harem eunuch cultivated ties.

SULTAN'S COMPANION

Beginning in the mid-1690s, Beshir seems to have advanced unusually quickly through the ranks of the unofficial palace eunuch hierarchy. The rapid trajectory of his career bolsters the theory that he was patronized by, and perhaps even brought to Istanbul by, Yapraksız Ali Agha. He appears to have become companion of the sultan – presumably Mustafa II (r. 1695–1703) – during Yapraksız Ali's tenure as chief eunuch. The sultan's companions were a rather loosely defined inner circle of palace functionaries who had more intimate access to the sultan than anyone but his immediate family and who were, consequently, enormously influential. During the fifteenth and sixteenth centuries, their numbers might include non-eunuch pages; by the early eighteenth century, however, they were almost without exception harem eunuchs. Among other things, these companions served as a means of communication between the sultan, when he was engaged in other parts of the palace, and his mother and favorite concubines. By this time, it had become routine for future chief harem eunuchs to hold the title companion early in their careers, and even to advance to the rank of chief companion, who oversaw eight to ten lower ranking companions, shortly before becoming chief eunuch.

THE SULTAN'S MOTHER

In addition to eunuchs, the residents of the palace harem included the sultan's mother, any of his sisters who had not been married off to high-ranking Ottoman officials, and his concubines. After the death in 1558 of Sultan Süleyman I's influential wife, sultans and crown princes no longer married; instead, imperial reproduction relied entirely on concubines, among whom a hierarchy of sultan's favorites obtained. Competition among the sultan's concubines could be fierce, particularly if more than one of them bore a son, for naturally every mother wanted her son to be first in line for the throne.

The sultan's mother, meanwhile, acquired unprecedented influence early in the seventeenth century, when the Ottomans discontinued the practice whereby the newly enthroned sultan had his brothers murdered. Around the same time, the practice of sending princes off to govern provinces in order to learn statecraft was likewise abandoned. Now, all Ottoman princes were raised in the harem and, on reaching maturity, resided in a special suite of rooms at the rear of the harem, known as the "Cage," until such time as they were called to the throne. In this new milieu, the sultan's mother was the single most important influence on the sultan's education and political outlook.

Gülnush Emetullah, Yusuf Agha, and the Köprülü reforms

Sultan Mustafa II, the sultan to whom Beshir Agha was companion, was the first son of Mehmed IV (r. 1648–87) to take the Ottoman throne, following the brief reigns of Mehmed's two half-brothers. Mustafa II's accession would therefore have marked a renewal of the influence of Rabia Gülnush Emetullah, the favorite concubine of Mehmed IV, who was Mustafa II's mother. As mother of the ruling sultan, Gülnush Emetullah was in a position to influence the selection of the chief harem eunuch and thus to have a hand in the chief eunuch's connections both within the palace and outside, even to as distant a province as Egypt. It is quite possible that she played a role in Yapraksız Ali's restoration to the imperial palace and that, therefore, she was indirectly responsible for Beshir Agha's palace career. As the chief influence on Mustafa II's upbringing and education, she would certainly have vetted his circle of companions early in his sultanate. Beshir, in any case, exercised a great deal of influence on Mustafa's successor, his brother Ahmed III, while the latter was still a prince. This he can have done only with the sultan's mother's acquiescence.

Well before she became the mother of a future sultan, Gülnush had demonstrated an intense interest in the Holy Cities pious foundations and the chief eunuch who oversaw them. In 1678, she founded an enormous pious endowment of her own for Mecca. This foundation drew its revenues from four carefully selected villages in Egypt, as well as from Cairo's Nile port of Bulaq. The endowment deed specifies as superintendent the then chief eunuch Yusuf Agha (tenure 1671–87). Ultimately, the endowment took advantage of Yusuf Agha's distinctive relationship with Egypt, which marks something of a turning point in the institutional history of the chief harem eunuch. Both as chief harem eunuch and after his exile to Cairo in 1687, Yusuf participated as no harem eunuch had done before in the household politics of Ottoman Egypt. He certainly played a role in selecting the villages to be endowed to Gülnush Emetullah's foundation, and possibly in assigning their tax farms to provincial grandees with whom he enjoyed close ties. In addition, he surely knew Ismail Bey, the chief financial officer who, as noted in chapter 3, may have been Beshir's patron in Cairo, and Ismail's father-in-law, the influential regimental commander; indeed, he indirectly supported Egypt's Faqari faction, in which both Ismail and his father-in-law played leading roles. In some respects, Yusuf Agha's political influence in both Egypt and Istanbul foreshadows that of Beshir Agha himself.

It is probably no coincidence, furthermore, that Yusuf Agha's term as chief harem eunuch coincides with the era of reforms under the father-and-son grand viziers, or chief ministers, of the Köprülü family: Köprülü Mehmed Pasha (term 1656–61) and Köprülü Fazıl Ahmed Pasha (term 1661–76). The Köprülüs' attempts to reform the empire's finances and military administration reached from the Ottoman provinces, where they appointed governors and other key officials from their own households, to the bowels of the imperial palace. They appointed their own clients as chief harem eunuch and made life uncomfortable for chief eunuchs who did not enjoy this status. At least one chief eunuch who was not linked to them in this fashion actually requested exile to Cairo, knowing that the Köprülüs would not tolerate his remaining in the imperial capital, where he might have attempted to counter their strategies. In this context, it seems likely that Yusuf Agha was a Köprülü protégé.

Although members of the Köprülu family occupied the office of grand vizier sporadically well into the eighteenth century, their influence never equaled that of their seventeenth-century forebears. Nonetheless, the Köprülü reforms left a lasting mark on the harem eunuch hierarchy and would influence the trajectory of Beshir Agha's own palace career as much as any of the sultan's mother's actions. In an attempt to rein in harem expenditures, which formed a substantial portion of overall palace outlays, the Köprülü grand viziers appear to have promoted a career pattern whereby the treasurer of the palace harem routinely advanced to the office of chief eunuch. Beshir Agha took the first step along this career path when, in 1707, he advanced from chief companion to harem treasurer.

THE "EDIRNE INCIDENT" (1703)

By this time, Sultan Mustafa II had been overthrown in the 1703 revolt that in Ottoman chronicles typically goes by the understated name of "the Edirne Incident." Since Mehmed IV's reign, the sultan and his retinue had preferred to reside and conduct business in the Balkan city of Edirne (Adrianople), situated in the Thracian plain northwest of Istanbul, near what is now Turkey's border with Bulgaria. While the city provided a forward position against the enemy Habsburg Empire, the surrounding countryside provided exceptional hunting, of which Mehmed IV, nicknamed "Mehmed the Hunter," was inordinately fond. To a large extent, the rebellion resulted from the frustrations of soldiery in Istanbul who resented both the court's relocation and the cessation of military operations against the Habsburgs. The Ottomans had besieged the Habsburg capital, Vienna, for two months in 1683, only to suffer defeat at the hands of Polish relief forces. Summer rains and mud turned the Ottoman retreat from Vienna into a disastrous rout, by the end of which the Ottomans had lost Hungary. A string of further defeats followed until, in 1699, the Ottomans signed the humiliating Treaty of Karlowitz, wherein they, for the first time, recognized the Habsburgs as an equal power.

During the "Edirne Incident," nonetheless, hostility centered on the empire's chief religious official, the supreme Muslim jurisconsult, who was notorious for appointing his relatives to high religious offices despite their lack of qualification and who was believed, in addition, to have provided religious justification for the peace treaty with the Habsburgs. The jurisconsult was executed as a result of this rebellion, while the grand vizier was deposed and given the governorship of Egypt as a sort of consolation prize. Mustafa II, meanwhile, was obliged to relinquish the throne in favor of his younger brother, who became Ahmed III.

Throughout this ordeal, remarkably, Beshir Agha continued as sultan's companion. This may have had much to do with Gülnush Emetullah, mother of both the deposed and the newly enthroned sultan, although she is not known to have played an active role in the rebellion or its resolution. She remained in the harem in Topkapı Palace in Istanbul throughout her elder son's reign, as, therefore, did most of the harem eunuchs, including Beshir. The fact that they remained in Istanbul, instead of going to Edirne with Sultan Mustafa, surely contributed to their ability to weather the crisis. Beshir's patron, Yapraksız Ali Agha, had been deposed from the office of chief harem eunuch and exiled to Egypt (for good this time) three years earlier. Ahmed III, for his part, transferred his base of operations back to Topkapı.

HAREM TREASURER

Four years after the "Edirne Incident," in 1707, Beshir Agha was promoted to harem treasurer, the stepping-stone to the post of chief harem eunuch. In the absence of Yapraksız Ali, we may conjecture that his promotion resulted from the skill he had shown as companion, as well as, no doubt, encouragement from Gülnush Emetullah. In this position, however, he was to run afoul of the grand vizier Chorlulu Ali Pasha.

In the aftermath of the Vienna debacle and with the end of the era of Köprülü reforms, the early eighteenth century was a time of great uncertainty in the grand vizierate. A series of grand viziers served very brief terms, in some cases less than a year; summary dismissals and even executions for perceived policy failures were common. In this atmosphere, Chorlulu Ali Pasha managed to be more effective than most other grand viziers of this period, yet even he was vulnerable to shifts in the climate of opinion in the palace. The son of a landholder from the central Anatolian district of Chorlu, Chorlulu Ali was appointed ceremonial weapons-bearer to Sultan Mustafa II in 1700 by one of the later Köprülü grand viziers. In this position, he attempted to promote such basic reforms as pruning the palace's bloated payroll and encouraging promotion by merit rather than by seniority or connections; he was opposed, however, by another grand vizier and by the nepotistic chief jurisconsult who later came to grief in the Edirne Incident. Emerging unscathed from the Edirne

Incident, Chorlulu Ali re-ascended the rungs of palace influence under Ahmed III, finally receiving the grand vizierate in 1706. He was suspicious of palace spending, which seemed to be mushrooming as Ahmed III indulged in baroque excesses. Chorlulu Ali apparently believed that the women of the imperial harem and their eunuch guards participated in, or at least encouraged, this spending. In a fit of reforming zeal, he attempted to subvert the entire harem eunuch establishment, and to that end ordered the governor of Egypt to cease importing young African eunuchs. His attempt did not succeed. Meanwhile, he had chosen to support Russia against the Swedes at a time when the Ottomans were at war with Russia and, in fact, had come close to capturing Tsar Peter the Great. His perceived Russophilia led to his execution in 1711.

Harem eunuchs were only slightly less vulnerable than grand viziers to shifts in the political winds during these tumultuous years. In 1713, under one of Chorlulu Ali's successors, Beshir Agha was exiled to Cyprus along with the then chief harem eunuch Uzun ("Tall") Süleyman Agha. This may have had to do with the new Ottoman offensive against Venice, as a result of which the Ottomans, by taking the southern Greek mainland in 1715, captured the last of Venice's possessions in the Aegean Sea. The harem eunuchs may have been regarded as having uncomfortably close ties to Venetian merchants, who purveyed some of the trinkets mentioned above, as well as the more costly luxury goods to be described in chapter 7. More likely, however, the perennial problem of unrestrained harem expenditures was the immediate trigger for this banishment. Exile, we must remember, was less a dire ruination than an almost routine lull in a palace career. Beshir probably expected that he would one day return to Istanbul.

Postscript: Moralı Beshir Agha (tenure 1746–52)

Despite his exile, Beshir Agha's advancement to harem treasurer – the last palace office he would hold before ascending to the post of chief harem eunuch – set a key precedent. Years later, on his death, he was succeeded as chief harem eunuch by the eunuch whom he himself, while chief eunuch, had appointed harem treasurer: Moralı Beshir Agha. His successor's sobriquet, Moralı ("from the Morea," i.e., the southern Greek mainland), derived from his initially having been the slave of the future governor of the Morea, who presented him to the future Sultan Mahmud I (r. 1730–54) when the latter was still a prince. Moralı Beshir became close to Mahmud and attained the rank of sultan's companion when Mahmud ascended the throne in 1730. Thus, his entrance into palace service and proximity to the new sultan do not seem to have depended on el-Hajj Beshir's patronage. Rather, el-Hajj Beshir may have seen fit to promote him because of his intimacy with the sultan. El-Hajj Beshir knew very well, however, that this promotion virtually guaranteed that Moralı Beshir would be the next chief harem eunuch.

5

EXILE IN CYPRUS AND EGYPT

CYPRUS

El-Hajj Beshir Agha was exiled to Cyprus in 1713 in the company of chief eunuch Uzun Süleyman Agha. Uzun Süleyman, who seems to have been a particular favorite of Sultan Ahmed III's mother, Gülnush Emetullah, remained on Cyprus until his death in 1715. Coincidentally, Gülnush Emetullah died that same year. Beshir Agha may well have stayed on Cyprus with Uzun Süleyman until his death; it is impossible to tell.

The Ottomans had conquered Cyprus from the Venetians in 1570. It was their last significant naval victory before the destruction of the Ottoman fleet at Lepanto in 1571; still, it affirmed Ottoman naval efficacy, the more so since the fleet was rebuilt by 1573. Although Cyprus would remain under Ottoman rule until the late nineteenth century, when it was added to the British Empire, Ottoman attempts to turn it into a prosperous province yielded decidedly mixed results. Land in many parts of the island was swampy and, consequently, malarial; the Ottoman central authority resorted to compulsory population transfer to populate the island so as to provide an Ottoman presence, as well as an agricultural and fiscal base. Despite these efforts, Cyprus remained a place of banishment for criminals and political exiles throughout its history under Ottoman rule. The time that Beshir Agha spent there cannot have been a particularly happy one.

EGYPT

*The harem eunuch's agent (***wakil***)*

Sometime between 1713 and 1716, however, Beshir was sent to Egypt, which since the mid-seventeenth century had been the most common place of exile for deposed harem eunuchs. In Cairo, he either already had or speedily acquired an agent (*wakil*) named Hasan Agha. This sort of agent to a palace eunuch was a figure of singular importance. To understand his significance, a brief examination of the term *wakil* and the institution to which it refers is useful.

The term *wakil* comes from the Arabic root *w-k-l*, having the sense of "to represent." The form of representation in question, however, could vary widely. One encounters *wakil*s quite frequently in the records of Muslim law courts during the Ottoman period, for women in particular often empowered *wakil*s to represent them in court. (Interestingly, these *wakil*s, while usually male, were usually *not* the husbands or other male relatives of the women concerned – perhaps because these women were all too familiar with their male relatives' weaknesses and preferred not to risk their representation in court!) The transfer of representational authority to the *wakil* was itself registered in the court record; in this case, therefore, this transfer closely resembled a power of attorney. Outside of the Muslim law courts, the *wakil* appears most frequently as a commercial agent: someone who handles sales and purchases of merchandise and property for the person who empowers him. This seems to have been, in large part, the sort of activity in which the *wakil* of a harem eunuch engaged.

*Wakil*s were seemingly indispensable to harem eunuchs even relatively early in their careers. A *wakil* had to be someone who genuinely had the harem eunuch's interests, professional and personal, at heart and who could be trusted implicitly not only to serve those interests but also to make independent decisions, such as the decision to purchase or sell property, in pursuit of those interests even without the harem eunuch's direct oversight. A slave or client of the harem eunuch who had been reared in his household and whose career he had personally nurtured would obviously have made the best choice for *wakil*. Beshir Agha's *wakil* at the time of his removal to Cairo, Hasan Agha, is described in a document from Cairo's Muslim law court archives as an officer in one of the two elite regiments of soldiery attached to the Egyptian governor's council. Since such officers were often appointed from Istanbul, he may indeed have been such a client to Beshir, yet it is impossible to be certain.

There appears to have been a range of *wakil*s who served the harem eunuch throughout his career. The culmination of the *wakil* profession seems to have been the permanent representative of the chief harem eunuch in Egypt, who will be discussed in detail in chapter 9.

By the late seventeenth century, exiled harem eunuchs and their agents had turned the neighborhood surrounding Birkat al-Fil, Cairo's "Elephant Pond" just west of the citadel – so-called because its shape resembled that of an elephant's head and trunk – into a veritable eunuch quarter. The pond was surrounded by mansions owned by eunuchs and provincial grandees; one passageway was even known as "The Place of the Eunuchs' Residence-Palace." Since eunuchs, like other political grandees in the palace and in the Ottoman provinces, acquired clients, even an exiled eunuch in Cairo might be surrounded by an entourage of such clients, both imported from Istanbul and acquired in Egypt. A eunuch might "bequeath" his house to one of his clients by endowing it to a personal pious foundation which the client would administer. Houses of deceased eunuchs, meanwhile, were occasionally used as places of house arrest for governors deposed by Egypt's grandees. Such houses were typically built or purchased under the supervision of an agent, or *wakil*.

Beshir Agha's agent, Hasan Agha, acquired a residence for him in the eunuch-heavy neighborhood around Birkat al-Fil. Adjacent to a residence belonging to Uzun Süleyman, with whom Beshir had been exiled to Cyprus, this house had been the residence of a governor of Egypt at the end of the sixteenth century and had since passed through the hands of various officials attached to the governor's council, as well as those of various military officers; its most recent occupant had been one Kıbrıslı, or "Cypriot." This and the fact that the house was next-door to Uzun Süleyman's residence cannot have been mere coincidence; clearly, Beshir's quarters had been arranged by his agent while Beshir was still on Cyprus, no doubt through this Cypriot connection in Cairo. The property included not only upstairs and downstairs living quarters but also a stable, several storerooms, and three shops. Beshir, or rather his agent, ultimately endowed this property as the eunuch's personal pious foundation. Beshir himself was to administer the endowment during his lifetime, after which supervision would pass to the oldest of his manumitted slaves. When the last of these died, the property would be assigned to the Holy Cities foundations. This legal strategy allowed Beshir not only to provide for himself during his sojourn in Cairo but also to ensure the welfare of his clients. Ultimately, it dovetailed neatly with the chief harem eunuch's attachment to the Holy Cities foundations.

Beshir's fountain in Cairo

In 1713, Beshir Agha commissioned his agent Hasan Agha to build a fountain in Cairo. This particular fountain was not a simple drinking fountain or a fountain for ritual ablutions before the five daily Muslim prayers, but a structure known as a *sabil-kuttab* in Arabic; it took the form of a Qur'an school (*kuttab*) over a public drinking fountain (*sabil*) which provided water to anyone who wanted it. An attendant on the lower floor of the structure drew water from an underground cistern and filled metal cups, which he passed to thirsty passersby through an opening in the metal grillework surrounding the fountain. Since the Qur'an urges Muslims to provide water to the thirsty, constructing such a fountain was a pious act for which the structure's founder could expect to be rewarded in heaven.

The fountain would probably have required several years to build and a substantial investment in stone, wood, glass, tile, metal pipes, and other building materials, to say nothing of construction labor. Hasan Agha remained in Cairo to oversee construction of the fountain when Beshir was named chief of the eunuchs guarding the Prophet's tomb in Medina, and may have continued there when

Beshir was recalled to Istanbul as chief harem eunuch in 1716. He apparently supervised all the requirements for the fountain while his patron remained in Medina and Istanbul, although Beshir may well have received a progress report en route from Medina back to Istanbul. The resulting structure still stands near Sultan Mahmud I's theological college, in Cairo's Azbakiyya district, just east of the Nile. The importance of such architectural monuments will be discussed in chapter 10.

Relations with Egypt's grandees

How long Beshir Agha stayed in Cairo at this juncture is unknown; he was there for perhaps a year or two at most. We do know that he lived in the house that his agent Hasan Agha had purchased for him on the shores of Birkat al-Fil; only a decade or so later would elite residences begin to migrate northwest to Azbakiyya.

By 1713, Beshir's ostensible "master" and possible first owner, the long-time chief financial officer of Egypt, Ismail Bey, was dead, as were the two military commanders who, with him, had dominated Egypt during the 1690s. The province was still struggling through the aftermath of a brutal civil war among the military-administrative cadres which had begun in 1711. Ultimately, the conflict would take the form of an unusually violent vendetta between the Faqaris and Qasimis, the two rival factions that had dominated Egypt for the past seven decades. As a client, if not the former slave, of Ismail Bey, Beshir Agha might have been expected to favor the Faqari faction, of which his patron had been a leader. However, he also had ties to the longtime leader of the Qasimi faction, as well as the young firebrand poised to dominate the Qasimi faction following this elderly leader's death. The civil war, in any case, signaled a generational shift within Egypt's military-administrative echelons, as well as a shift in the relationship of the two factions. The old day-to-day *modus vivendi* of the factions, whereby factional leaders, at least in Cairo, were content to maintain a balance of power, seems to have been broken. Now, factional antagonism reached unprecedented heights while bloody intra-factional rivalry loomed. Under these circumstances, the disposition of the tax farms connected to the Holy Cities foundations would have been a chief concern of the chief harem eunuch and of Beshir Agha as harem treasurer. What, if anything, he did to come to grips with this issue while in Egypt, however, is unknown.

6

CHIEF OF THE TOMB EUNUCHS IN MEDINA

Like the seventeenth-century chief harem eunuch Yusuf Agha, who, as noted in chapter 4, was unusually active in Egyptian politics, Beshir went from Egypt to Medina to serve as "Master of the Prophetic Sanctuary," or chief of the corps of eunuchs who guarded the Prophet Muhammad's tomb. As noted in chapter 2, this eunuch guard seems to have been instituted sometime during the twelfth century after the overthrow of Shi'ite Fatimid rule in the Holy Cities. To avoid confusion over the competing Sunni and Shi'ite claims to the Prophet's tomb and positions on the Prophet's legacy, a brief digression on Shi'ism is in order.

SHI'ISM

Sunni Muslims, who today comprise the vast majority of the world's Muslim population, differ from the various Shi'ite subsects over the critical issue of how Muhammad's successor as leader of the Muslim community should have been chosen. Since Muhammad had no surviving sons at the time of his death in 632 and had not unequivocally designated a successor, a small group of community elders selected his father-in-law, Abu Bakr, as the first caliph, or successor. This doctrine of community consensus in the selection of the caliph is the defining feature of Sunni Islam. Shi'ites, in contrast, believe that Muhammad, shortly before his death, had designated his cousin and son-in-law, Ali, to succeed him, and that the true caliph – or Imam, in Shi'ite theological parlance – must be a descendant of Ali and the Prophet's daughter Fatima. Allegiance to descendants of Ali as the proper candidates for caliph is thus the defining feature of Shi'ism.

By Beshir Agha's time, of course, these disputes over the caliphate were over a millennium in the past. Nevertheless, the ancient disputes received new life in the sixteenth century with the rise of the Twelver Shi'ite Safavid dynasty in Iran and the renewed militancy of the Zaydi Shi'ite Imams of Yemen. These Shi'ite powers posed an ideological, as well as a geopolitical, threat to the Ottomans, since the Ottoman sultan had come to be recognized as caliph of the world's Sunni Muslims. This consensus seems to have developed gradually following the Ottoman conquest in 1516–17 of the Mamluk sultanate, which had not only ruled the Holy Cities of Mecca and Medina but had sheltered a descendant of the Abbasid caliphs in Cairo following the destruction of the Abbasids' empire by the Mongols in 1258.

The three chief subsects of Shi'a Islam differ over the descendants of Ali whom they recognize as Imams. The Twelvers, today the majority among Shi'ites and the subsect that predominates in Iran, are so called because they recognize a line of twelve Imams. They believe that the young son of the eleventh Imam, who died in the mid-ninth century C.E., exists in a state of occultation and will return at the end of time. Ismailis, or Seveners, recognize a different seventh Imam from the one recognized by Twelvers, and initially believed that the son of this seventh Imam was the last of the line and had gone into occultation. Many adherents of the sect came to support the Fatimid caliphate, founded by a self-proclaimed descendant of the seventh Imam, which took over North Africa, Egypt, Syria, and the Holy Cities of Mecca and Medina in the tenth century. Yemen's Ismaili population dates in large part to the Fatimid era, when a Fatimid-friendly Ismaili regime ruled Yemen. The smallest of the Shi'ite subsects, the Zaydis, do not recognize a fixed line of Imams but acknowledge any descendant of Ali's elder son Hasan or younger son Husayn who is learned in Islam and who demonstrates his ability to defend the community by taking power militarily. The subsect's name comes from Zayd, a great-grandson of Ali who rebelled against the Sunni Umayyad caliph in 740 and whom the Zaydis, unlike Twelvers or Ismailis, initially recognized as the fifth Shi'ite Imam. The Zaydi sect took root in Yemen in the late ninth century and has remained a force there ever since.

Following the overthrow of the Ismaili Fatimid caliphate in the late twelfth century, the families of descendants of the Prophet Muhammad who continued to dominate Mecca and Medina politically and religiously were Shi'ites of the Zaydi and Ismaili subsects, as was a large proportion of the resident populations of both cities. Shi'ites revere Muhammad as Sunnis do and hold his daughter Fatima, who is also buried in the Prophet's tomb complex, in special reverence as the wife of Ali and mother of the succeeding Shi'ite Imams. On the other hand, they object to the presence in the complex of the tombs of Abu Bakr and Umar, the first two caliphs recognized by Sunnis. The Shi'ites of Medina, to say nothing of the Zaydi Shi'ite Imams who dominated northern Yemen, resented Sunni control of the Prophet's tomb and the reverence for the two Sunni caliphs that it entailed.

The early Mamluk sultans, in the late thirteenth century, had made a concerted effort to shore up Sunni Islam in Medina, where they had faced a territorial and political challenge from the Zaydi Imam of northern Yemen. The eunuch guard was part of this effort since the eunuchs deterred Shi'ites from creating disturbances at the tomb. The Ottomans also faced a Zaydi challenge, as well as a challenge from the Twelver Shi'ites of Iran, although neither was ever as potent a threat to control of the Holy Cities themselves. Nonetheless, the Ottomans continued the Mamluk tradition of the eunuch tomb guard.

MEDINA

Sir Richard Francis Burton's two-volume *Personal Narrative of a Pilgrimage to al-Madinah and Meccah*, describing the author's 1853 pilgrimage, which he completed disguised as a wandering Muslim mystic from Anatolia, provides a detailed description of Medina and of the Prophet's mosque and tomb compound roughly 135 years after Beshir Agha presided over the corps of eunuchs there. Although Medina had certainly changed during that period, the scope of change to the city's physical layout was relatively minor. The city, situated in a plain set off by low basaltic hills to the east and west and palm groves to the south, was apparently walled only in the early nineteenth century; prior to about 1812, it was ringed only with earthworks, pierced by four gates: the Egyptian Gate, facing west; the Syrian Gate, facing northwest; the Gate of Hospitality, facing north; and the Friday Gate, facing east. The Ottomans constructed a fort adjoining the Syrian Gate to the west, and beyond this, a sort of suburb grew up, consisting largely of Ottoman soldiers' barracks and the residences of local notables. At the southwestern edge of this suburb was the Grain Gate, through which, presumably, grain from Upper Egyptian villages endowed to the Holy Cities foundations was brought into Medina.

THE MOSQUE OF THE PROPHET

The Prophet's mosque is situated in the eastern part of the city. This mosque was the first ever constructed in Islamic history and the one used regularly by the Prophet Muhammad himself, yet by the eighteenth century little trace remained of the humble structure that the Prophet must have frequented. The first three caliphs, or successors to Muhammad as leaders of the Muslim community recognized by Sunni Muslims, and successive Muslim dynasties, beginning with the Umayyads (661–750), had greatly expanded and embellished the mosque out of reverence for the man who founded it. The structure with which Beshir Agha would become intimately familiar dated from the reign of the Umayyad caliph al-Walid (r. 705–15), the same caliph who commissioned the Great Mosque of Damascus and who, in many respects, established the prototype for mosque architecture. Although the Ottomans undertook a number of repairs and additions to the mosque in the late sixteenth century, they retained the basic structure of al-Walid's day.

Unlike Ottoman mosques of the fifteenth and sixteenth centuries, which were, to the extent possible in a given city, built on relatively elevated ground so as to achieve visual dominance, the Prophet's mosque is on a level with other buildings in Medina, so that, as Burton puts it, "there is no outer front, no general prospect" (Burton 1893, vol. 1, p. 307). Architecturally, the mosque is of the "hypostyle" type common to the early Islamic period, centering on a large rectangular courtyard that serves as an extension of the columned interior prayer space. In this respect, the Prophet's mosque resembles far more the Umayyad Mosque in Damascus or the Great Mosque of Córdoba, Spain, than it does a "classical" Ottoman mosque. This courtyard, however, boasted a stand of palm trees in its center which was popularly believed to be the garden of the Prophet's daughter Fatima, wife of Ali. In actual fact, one of the early tomb eunuchs had planted these palm trees, and the corps of eunuchs extracted income from the sale of the dates produced by these trees.

The Umayyad caliph al-Walid also endowed a number of pious foundations for the mosque's upkeep; these were enlarged by the Mamluk sultans and by the Ottomans, both of whom founded a number of endowments of their own. The great Ottoman sultan Süleyman "the Magnificent" (r. 1520–66) paved over the area known as the "Garden," which separates the mosque and tomb, with white marble tiles, which are today still one of the striking features of the tomb's surroundings. Keeping the mosque and tomb well-maintained and equipped, to say nothing of managing the budget for this upkeep, was a demanding task indeed, and it was this task that the chief tomb eunuch oversaw.

THE TOMB OF THE PROPHET

The Prophet's tomb lies directly to the east of the mosque, on the site of what was once his house after he migrated to Medina in 622 C.E. This layout hints at how humble and even *ad hoc* the original arrangements for the establishment of the first Muslim community in Medina must have been. Having established a place of worship and consultation on the spot where his she-camel halted, Muhammad resided in a modest dwelling just beside it. Abutting his house was that of his daughter Fatima. When Muhammad died in 632, he was buried under the floor of his house, as was the custom in seventh-century Arabia. His favorite wife, Aisha, only 18 at the time of his death, continued to live in the house until her own death in 678. Her father, Abu Bakr, became the first caliph, or successor to Muhammad as community leader, in 632; when he died two years later, he was likewise buried under the floor of the Prophet's house, as was the second caliph, Umar, who was assassinated in 644. According to the biographical traditions of the Prophet, his family, and his companions, following Umar's death, Aisha had a wall built between the living quarters of the house and the space occupied by the graves, for, in keeping with the modesty and dignity associated with the wives of the Prophet, she did not wish to appear unveiled before an unrelated male (namely, Umar), even if he were dead. A fourth, empty grave was thought to be for Jesus, considered a prophet by Muslims, when he returns at the end of time in the company of the messianic figure recognized by many Sunni Muslims. Aisha herself, although she died in Medina in this very house, was not buried in this chamber but in the cemetery to the east of the mosque where the Prophet's wives were buried, as were other relatives and companions of the Prophet. Muhammad's daughter Fatima, who died several months after her father, was, in contrast, buried beneath what had been her house; thus, her tomb chamber abuts that of the Prophet.

Over a quarter century after Aisha's death, the Umayyad caliph al-Walid constructed the mosque of the Prophet more or less in the basic form it retains today. A later Umayyad caliph sealed the tomb chamber of the Prophet and the first two caliphs, along with that of Fatima, within an enclosure open only near the roof, thus cutting off access to the Prophet's tomb by all but a handful of pious figures deputized to enter the tomb chamber to repair damage caused by collapsing walls or to remove the corpses of small animals which had accidentally fallen into the chamber. In 1256, however, this enclosure was destroyed by fire. The first Mamluk sultan, who came to power in 1260, replaced it with an ornamental wooden screen around the chambers. This was later replaced by a more durable brass structure, pierced with three gates and two windows. Visitors to the tomb could now come no closer to the Prophet's cenotaph than this barrier, although one of the windows in the encircling wall did look onto the space directly above the cenotaph, where hung a jeweled ornament known as the "pearl constellation." In the latter part of the fifteenth century, the Mamluk sultan Qaytbay (r. 1468–96) extensively restored and renovated the mosque, which had been damaged by lightning in the thirteenth century; to his era belong most of the mosque's minarets and gates. It was Qaytbay who ordered the construction of the green dome that covers the Prophet's tomb today.

THE TOMB EUNUCHS

Immediately in front of the tomb enclosure, abutting Fatima's chamber and facing toward the mosque, was the porch where a number of the "tomb eunuchs" sat. They were there to protect the tomb from unwelcome intruders, notably Shi'ites, who, as noted above, resented the presence in the compound of the tombs of Abu Bakr and Umar. While Sunnis recognize Abu Bakr and Umar as the first two caliphs, Shi'ites regard them as usurpers of Ali's right to the caliphate, insisting instead that the Prophet had, in truth, designated Ali as his successor in leading the Muslim community.

The Mamluk sultans erected the aforementioned barrier and reinforced the eunuch guard not only to prevent aberrant, non-normative behavior at the Prophet's tomb but also as a counter-measure to the claims of the Zaydi Shi'ite Imams of Yemen on the holy sites of Medina. Not only did the Zaydi Imams present an ideological challenge to the Sunni Mamluks; they posed a continual military threat to Mamluk control of Mecca and Medina as well, and nearly succeeded in occupying Mecca in the early fourteenth century. In addition to the Zaydi threat, the Mamluks sought to counter the lingering influence of Ismaili Shi'ite populations resident in the region of the Holy Cities.

The Ottomans faced similar Shi'ite challenges. During the sixteenth and seventeenth centuries, when the Twelver Shi'ite Safavid Empire established its authority in Iran and challenged the Ottomans militarily in Iraq, Shi'ite pilgrims from the Safavid domains would have been regarded as potential threats to the security of the tomb precinct. During the same period, the rebellion of a Zaydi Shi'ite Imam in Yemen, followed by the Ottoman ouster from Yemen by a succeeding dynasty of Zaydi Imams, abruptly revived the Zaydi threat to the Holy Cities and would have further highlighted the importance of the eunuch guard. Even in the mid-nineteenth century, some 130 years after the collapse of the Safavid Empire and two decades before the Ottomans reoccupied Yemen, Sir Richard Francis Burton remarks that Shi'ites visiting the Prophet's tomb often attempted to throw rubbish into the tombs of Abu Bakr and Umar. The intimidating phalanx of eunuchs would have acted as a check on such behavior; indeed, Burton describes the eunuchs he encountered as beating perceived malefactors with canes.

With very few exceptions, only members of the corps of tomb eunuchs were allowed to enter the chamber in which the Prophet's tomb lay. They might admit outsiders, as they saw fit, into the passageway between the porch and the tomb chamber proper; Burton implies that this was typically in exchange for a substantial sum of money or an expensive gift. This passageway also housed the treasury of the mosque and tomb, in keeping with the venerable practice, already visible in the early eighth-century Umayyad Mosque in Damascus, of placing the treasury in the innermost sanctum, which by definition was more closely guarded and therefore more secure than the surrounding area. The Mamluks had instituted this policy of restricted access to the Prophet's tomb to keep the frequently antagonistic population of thirteenth-century Medina in check. By the Ottoman period, the eunuch guard had become something of a hallowed institution; it would not be abolished until the Saudis took over the Holy Cities in the early twentieth century, at which time the remaining tomb eunuchs were pensioned off.

Number and duties of tomb eunuchs

The number of eunuchs employed in the Holy Cities was far smaller than that employed at the Ottoman imperial palace in Istanbul:

Burton reports 120 at the Prophet's mosque and tomb in Medina, and roughly eighty at the Great Mosque, housing the sacred cubical structure known as the Ka'ba, in Mecca; in contrast, as noted in chapter 2, some ten times that number inhabited Topkapı Palace by the end of the sixteenth century. By the seventeenth century, the tomb eunuchs appear to have been overwhelmingly African, whereas the Mamluk sultanate had employed a mixture of eunuchs from the Caucasus, eastern Africa, and southern India. As in the palace, so at the tomb of the Prophet in Medina, a hierarchy of eunuchs obtained. At the pinnacle of this hierarchy stood the "Master of the Prophetic Sanctuary" himself, who had the authority to appoint or dismiss all subordinate tomb eunuchs. Directly below him was the group of eunuchs who handled the finances of the Prophet's mosque and tomb, including chief and deputy treasurers and a number of scribes, or accountants. The bulk of the tomb eunuchs, however, were employed in physical tasks around the mosque and tomb. The highest-ranking of these acted as doormen for the mosque, while the next rank swept the mosque's interior, and the lowest-ranking cleaned dirt, rubbish, and other impurities from the mosque and tomb precincts while acting as veritable sergeants-at-arms, beating people who fell asleep in the mosque, as well as those found behaving inappropriately in the mosque or around the tomb.

A small number of this corps of eunuchs sat in the "Eunuchs' Porch" fronting the tomb and warded off any ill-intentioned visitors to the tomb while simultaneously ensuring that the behavior of the well-intentioned remained within the limits of propriety, without becoming frenzied or overwrought. Although as chief tomb eunuch, Beshir Agha would have sat in the "Eunuchs' Porch" for the sake of ceremony and intimidation, many of the eunuchs who surrounded him in the porch must have been younger, more junior members of the corps of tomb eunuchs, in particular men young and strong enough to confront the threat of physical violence from Shi'ites and other antagonists, or the sheer physical fervor of devoted Muslims of various sorts who simply wanted to enter the tomb chamber, or at least to get as close to it as possible, in order to benefit from the Prophet's spiritual aura.

The tomb covering

The tomb eunuchs were responsible, among other things, for covering the Prophet's cenotaph with a decorative cloth, similar to, though on a much smaller scale than, the richly embroidered cloth with which the cubical stone structure known as the Ka'ba is covered. Both these coverings were transported to the Holy Cities by the two mammoth pilgrimage caravans which the Ottomans sponsored each year: one from Cairo, the other from Damascus. While the Ka'ba's covering came to Mecca each year with the Egyptian caravan, the covering for the Prophet's tomb was embroidered in Damascus and carried to Medina by the Damascus caravan. Unlike the Ka'ba covering, which was typically of costly black material, embroidered with Qur'anic verses in gold, the covering for the Prophet's tomb could be of black, green, or purple silk and was embroidered with inscriptions in white or silver thread, typically arranged in zigzag lines. Like the Ka'ba's covering, it was prepared each year with the utmost care, and when removed, it was cut up into pieces which were then distributed to the eunuchs and other functionaries of the Prophet's mosque, as well as to various pilgrims. A group of eunuchs entered the tomb chamber at night during the pilgrimage season to cover the tomb with the new cloth; legend had it that they veiled their faces when performing this task, lest they be blinded by "the supernatural splendours which pour from the tomb" (Burton 1893, vol. 1, pp. 321–2, n. 2).

Palace eunuchs and tomb eunuchs

The chief tomb eunuch under the Mamluks was usually a veteran of Mamluk palace service; indeed, the move from the citadel in Cairo, where the Mamluk sultans held court, to the tomb of the Prophet was regarded as a sort of spiritual exaltation for the eunuch in question. It is worth noting in this connection that Ottoman eunuchs serving in Medina are reported by European observers to have had wives – typically former African or, occasionally, Caucasian slave girls – whereas palace eunuchs apparently had no such wives; this may have signified that the tomb eunuchs had figuratively overcome their eunuchhood by "going up" to Medina. In any case, the pattern of moving from palace to tomb eunuch was already well established before the Ottomans assumed control of the Holy Cities, and lower-ranking eunuchs from the imperial palace in Istanbul do seem occasionally to have been assigned to Medina.

As noted in chapter 6, the late seventeenth-century chief eunuch Yusuf Agha was the first Ottoman chief harem eunuch to be assigned to Medina; he, however, assumed his new post only after four years' exile in Cairo. Thus, Egypt was still very much a waystation between Istanbul and Medina for prospective chief tomb eunuchs. This circumstance no doubt resulted in large part from Egypt's continuing "special relationship" with the Holy Cities, whereby it provided the larger of the two annual pilgrimage caravans and ensured the provision of grain to the Holy Cities; the exiled chief eunuchs' status as former superintendents of the pious endowments for the Holy Cities must also have played a role in their occasional transfer from Cairo to Medina. At the same time, the ancient Mamluk tradition of sending eunuchs to Medina from Cairo may have been a lingering influence. Now, however, these eunuchs were typically former Topkapı Palace harem eunuchs. In any event, Beshir Agha was unique in serving as chief tomb eunuch before serving as chief harem eunuch. This pattern would never be repeated.

The Köprülü reforms in Medina

There is reason to believe that the chief tomb eunuch's fiscal role was paramount: that he served as the acting chief harem eunuch's "man on the spot" who ensured that revenues earmarked for the Holy Cities charitable foundations were actually being spent for that purpose. As of the late seventeenth century, the hierarchy of tomb eunuchs paralleled that of the Topkapı Palace eunuch hierarchy: directly subordinate to the chief tomb eunuch was a corps of fiscal overseers, in the same way that the chief harem eunuch's immediate subordinate, in the wake of the Köprülü reforms, was the harem treasurer. In these conditions, a former chief harem eunuch made the ideal chief tomb eunuch since, having both supervised the Holy Cities foundations and served as harem treasurer, he possessed the requisite administrative and fiscal experience. It seems likely, in fact, that the habit of reassigning exiled chief harem eunuchs to Medina was a direct consequence of the Köprülü grand viziers' reforms. In 1691, the above-mentioned Yusuf Agha became the first exiled chief harem eunuch to take up the post of chief tomb eunuch. He had served as chief harem eunuch at the height of the Köprülü reforms, and after he set the precedent, it became fairly routine for exiled chief harem eunuchs to assume leadership of the eunuchs guarding the Prophet's tomb. Indeed, this innovation may have been the brainchild of the younger son of the first Köprülü grand vizier, who was serving as grand vizier at the time of Yusuf's appointment to Medina. The new career trajectory would have strengthened the connection binding the acting chief harem eunuch, the exiled eunuch community in Egypt, and the tomb eunuchs in Medina, ultimately contributing to greater oversight of the Holy Cities by the central authority.

Furthermore, the chief tomb eunuch could play the sort of political role in the Arabian peninsula that the Köprülu grand viziers particularly valued. He could keep an eye on the *sharif* of Mecca, member of a family of descendants of the Prophet Muhammad who administered the Hijaz, the western coastal plain of the Arabian peninsula, on behalf of the Ottomans. Conflicts between rival claimants for this office were fairly common in Ottoman history and not infrequently entangled Ottoman troops on the way to Yemen or, after the Ottoman ouster from Yemen by the Zaydi Shi'ite Imam in 1636, troops protecting the pilgrimage caravan. If the chief tomb eunuch could contribute to peace among various candidates for *sharif* and to stability in the Holy Cities generally, then the pilgrimage benefited, as did the Holy Cities pious foundations and the imperial treasury. Here, the agendas of the chief tomb eunuch, the chief harem eunuch, and the Köprülü reformers all converged.

RELATIONS WITH MEDINA'S AND EGYPT'S NOTABLES

The posting to Medina would have allowed Beshir Agha to join the ranks of Medina's local notables, including wealthy and influential regional and long-distance merchants. As chief tomb eunuch, he would have had a substantial residence in Medina, quite separate from the mosque and tomb of the Prophet, where his duties were concentrated. Indeed, the presence in Medina of so many eunuchs attached to the tomb complex resulted in the coalescing of a eunuch quarter, not unlike the quarter of exiled eunuchs in Cairo. Medina's eunuch quarter stood next to one of the gates of the tomb complex, and the chief tomb eunuch's residence stood at the entrance to the quarter.

At the same time, Beshir's presence in Medina would have strengthened his ties to those grandees of Egypt who dominated the pilgrimage: specifically, the pilgrimage commander, who held the rank of *bey* (equivalent to a subprovincial governor), and the Janissary officers responsible for protecting the caravan en route from Cairo to Mecca and Medina. By 1715, these officers were typically members of a new household that had emerged from within the Faqari faction; this was the Qazdağlı household, founded by the regimental officer who had dominated Egypt in the late seventeenth century in conjunction with Beshir Agha's putative patron, Ismail Bey the chief financial officer, and Ismail's father-in-law. The Qazdağlıs used control of the pilgrimage, along with domination of Egypt's port customs and Red Sea shipping, to amass a fortune from the trade in Yemeni coffee, which had been introduced into Egypt and the rest of the Ottoman Empire in the sixteenth century. Since exiled chief harem eunuchs in Egypt appear to have taken great interest in this commerce, to the extent of making substantial investments in it, it is not unreasonable to assume that Beshir Agha likewise profited from the transit of coffee along the pilgrimage route during his tenure as chief tomb eunuch.

In this connection, the estate inventory of a leader of the Qazdağlı household during the 1730s is of considerable interest. This man became a leading officer in Egypt's Janissary regiment and, in 1736, was appointed protector of the pilgrimage caravan. Three years later, while encamped at Birkat al-Hajj, the "Pilgrim's Pond" just east of Cairo from where the caravan departed for the Sinai, he suffered some sort of respiratory attack – the result of a condition reportedly brought on by the shock of witnessing his master's assassination earlier that year – and died. An inventory of his estate was prepared by the governor's bureaucrats and preserved in the archives of Cairo's Muslim courts. According to the inventory, this Qazdağlı leader counted one "Beshir, the imperial harem eunuch," among his followers. It is unlikely that this was our Beshir, who was promoted to chief harem eunuch before this Qazdağlı leader had attained prominence; the reference must therefore be to another imperial harem eunuch named Beshir, possibly the third chief eunuch named Beshir, who attained the office in 1752 and who retired three years later to Cairo, where he seems to have owned a mansion in Azbakiyya, which had displaced Birkat al-Fil as the hub of elite residence. His inclusion in this Qazdağlı leader's estate inventory may reflect an emerging Qazdağlı strategy or, indeed, a strategy of Egypt's leading grandees as a whole: to patronize a harem eunuch so as to cultivate good relations with the palace in general and the acting chief harem eunuch in particular. In addition, the inventory illustrates the Qazdağlı leader's intensive involvement in the Red Sea coffee trade, from which his followers, including the "other" Beshir Agha, must also have profited. These commercial profits would have been an added benefit to harem eunuchs of affiliation with this household.

7

CHIEF EUNUCH OF THE TOPKAPI PALACE HAREM

Beshir Agha was the only Ottoman chief harem eunuch to have served as chief eunuch of the Prophet's tomb in Medina *before* assuming the post of chief eunuch of the imperial palace harem. In 1716, he was recalled from Medina to the palace and appointed to the latter office. He would have been about 60 years of age, a detail that illustrates the fact that chief harem eunuch was a post assumed relatively late in life, as the capstone of a long palace career. His pre-chief eunuch career was unusual in including a multi-year period of exile, as well as service in Medina.

RETURN TO ISTANBUL

To return to Istanbul from Medina, Beshir Agha accompanied the returning pilgrimage caravan back to Cairo, where he stayed for two additional months. He appears to have made the pilgrimage himself that year, and it may have been then that he acquired the honorific title el-Hajj, or "the Pilgrim" – although he may have made one or more earlier pilgrimages as well. After reaching Cairo, he would have gone down the Nile to Alexandria to take ship for the imperial capital. The pilgrimage that year occurred in November, and the sultanic order appointing Beshir chief harem eunuch reached him in Mecca at the end of that month. He returned to Cairo at the beginning of 1717 and waited to embark for Istanbul until April, a decision that made perfect sense as the prime sailing seasons were autumn and spring. (It was during this relatively brief stop in Cairo that Hasan Agha, the *wakil*, or agent, mentioned in chapter 5, endowed Beshir's residential property at Birkat al-Fil as a pious foundation.)

Although Beshir Agha's departure from Egypt and arrival in Istanbul would not have occasioned ceremonial processions on a par with those accompanying a new governor's arrival in Egypt or the return of a grand vizier from a military victory, they would have been important official occasions marked with some degree of ritual. Certainly the governor and grandees of Egypt, on the one hand, and the sultan and grand vizier, on the other, were fully aware when the new chief eunuch was under sail. During the previous century, this passage across the eastern Mediterranean had been perilous, not so much because of changeable weather as because of the risk of attack by Roman Catholic pirates, particularly members of the Knights of St John of Malta, who used Crete, then still under Venetian rule, as a base. Indeed, the first chief eunuch exiled to Egypt had been martyred when his ship was attacked by the Knights of St John in 1644. This incident allegedly triggered the Ottoman attempt to conquer Crete, which was launched in 1644 and dragged on for twenty-five years until troops under the second Köprülü grand vizier finally took Candia (present-day Heraklion) in 1669. This conquest rendered the passage far safer for subsequent exiled eunuchs and others.

Once through the Dardanelles and into the Sea of Marmara, Beshir Agha's galley would have docked at "Seraglio Point," a spit of land jutting into the confluence of the Bosphorus, the Sea of Marmara, and the Golden Horn near Topkapı Palace. There, it would have been met by various palace officials, probably including lower-ranking harem eunuchs. The aging eunuch, dressed in appropriate ceremonial attire (on which see below), would have disembarked and mounted a horse on which to ride the few kilometers to the palace.

RETURN TO THE HAREM

The harem of Topkapı Palace resembled an enclosed city within the palace walls, with its own peculiar layout, social hierarchy, and internal culture. By 1717, the African eunuchs enjoyed a long-established residential space and base of operations that more or less surrounded the women's quarters inside the harem. There, lower-ranking eunuchs lived in dormitory-like chambers while the chief eunuch inhabited a separate set of apartments. The eunuchs prayed in a mosque specially built for them within the harem precinct.

Beshir Agha must have found it strange indeed to return, as it were in triumph, to the place from which he had been exiled, in something resembling disgrace, just four years before. Surrounded by the entourage which he had brought from Cairo, as well as that which had greeted him at Seraglio Point, he would have ridden through the palace's First Court, outside the main gate, where the public were allowed to gather to present petitions, then through Topkapı's distinctive main gate, flanked by two pointed turrets. He was now inside the Second Court, where Janissaries and visiting foreign dignitaries might tread but where the public at large was unwelcome. His horse would then have veered slightly left, toward the black eunuchs' entrance of the enormous harem complex on the western side of the Second Court. It was no accident that this rather humble portal stood adjacent to the entrance to the quarters of the halberdiers, or "axemen," for the halberdiers were a corps of palace soldiery traditionally close to the chief harem eunuch.

Once through the eunuchs' entrance, Beshir would have dismounted in the "Courtyard of the Black Eunuchs," which contains a set of steps constructed specifically for this sort of mounted entrance. To the left of this courtyard were the quarters of the rank-and-file harem eunuchs, which consisted of two stories of small sleeping chambers over a common room, a coffee-making room, and several sitting rooms. The entire complex was heated by a tiled Turkish fireplace-cum-stove at the end of the corridor. To one side of these quarters was the small mosque which the harem eunuchs used.

Beyond the rank-and-file eunuchs' quarters lay the Ottoman princes' school and the quarters of the chief eunuch, where Beshir Agha was about to install himself for the next thirty years. The school and the chief eunuch's quarters were intimately connected, for the chief eunuch oversaw the early education of the princes, as well as that of the harem women. At the age of 5 or so, a prince was brought from the "Cage" at the rear of the harem complex, where, as noted in chapter 4, princes had customarily resided since the early seventeenth century, to the schoolroom next to the chief eunuch's quarters to be instructed by a tutor chosen by the sultan. Once the prince was circumcised, at the age of 11 to 13, he no longer attended this school but acquired his own household within the "Cage," with one of the harem eunuchs as a sort of combination tutor–household manager. In this fashion, the Ottoman harem eunuchs took on duties not unlike those of the eunuchs of the Mamluk sultanate, who oversaw the education of young mamluks in the barracks of that empire's sultan.

Beshir Agha's new quarters consisted of a suite of small rooms, including bedroom, lavatory, coffee room, and smoking room. Clearly, the harem eunuchs partook of the widespread affinity in Ottoman society for coffee, which, as noted in chapter 6 in connection with Egypt, had been introduced from Yemen in the sixteenth century and in which eunuchs exiled to Egypt invested heavily. That they smoked is also no surprise. Tobacco, introduced from the New World not long after coffee arrived from Yemen, was equally widespread, and particularly popular among soldiers and palace guards. Miniature paintings from the era of Süleyman the Magnificent already show Janissary officers at the palace holding long pipes.

Across the "Courtyard of the Black Eunuchs" from the chief eunuch's apartments lay those of the harem treasurer, which Beshir would have occupied just before his exile to Cyprus four years earlier. Next to these were the apartments of the chief sultan's companion, a eunuch office slightly below that of harem treasurer; in all probability, Beshir had occupied these apartments during the late 1690s and the first years of the eighteenth century, when he exerted such great influence over the future Sultan Ahmed III. In the course of Beshir's lengthy tenure as chief eunuch, these two posts would be filled by his protégés.

At the end of the courtyard of the eunuchs lay the entrance to the harem proper, and just beyond that the extensive suite – much larger than the chief eunuch's suite – of the sultan's mother. When Beshir Agha returned to the palace in 1717, this suite may well have been unoccupied, for the mother of Ahmed III, Gülnush Emetullah, had died two years before. Since Beshir's exile to Cyprus, furthermore, two additional chief harem eunuchs had come and gone.

VIZIER MAKER

Gülnush Emetullah's demise may have created a vacuum among Sultan Ahmed III's closest advisers which Beshir Agha now seized the opportunity to fill. He now became "vizier maker," personally selecting for the post of grand vizier palace functionaries whom he could ensure would not challenge his own authority. The grand vizier at the time of Beshir's accession as chief eunuch had earlier been the functionary who affixed the sultan's seal to official documents. As such, he represented the new trend in the eighteenth century of grand viziers who had come up through the palace bureaucracy rather than through the military hierarchy. Although Beshir Agha would promote grand viziers who followed this career trajectory, he nonetheless maneuvered to depose this particular grand vizier within a year of his own appointment as chief eunuch. He then proved instrumental in promoting to the post of grand vizier Nevshehirli Ibrahim Pasha, a bureaucrat from the central Anatolian city of Nevshehir who had recently married Ahmed III's daughter and thus attained the pivotal status of imperial son-in-law.

NEVSHEHIRLI IBRAHIM PASHA

Nevshehirli Ibrahim had grown close to Ahmed III while the latter was still a crown prince; when Ahmed took the throne in 1703, Ibrahim was named secretary to Chief Eunuch Küchük ("Small") Abdurrahman Agha, then to his successor Uzun ("Tall") Süleyman Agha, with whom Beshir was exiled to Cyprus in 1713. Ibrahim himself was banished to Edirne (which, as noted in chapter 4, had been abandoned as a sultanic residence in the wake of the 1703 "Edirne Incident") several years earlier as a result of palace infighting. Restored to Ahmed III's favor in 1715, he participated in the reconquest of southern Greece from Venice, then in the unsuccessful defense of Belgrade against the Habsburgs. It was mainly he who persuaded the sultan to accept the peace negotiations that led to the Treaty of Passarowitz between the Ottomans and the Habsburgs in 1718. He attained the grand vizierate in large part because of this diplomatic success.

THE TULIP ERA

Nevshehirli Ibrahim Pasha receives credit for launching the so-called "Tulip Era," a period of efflorescence in Ottoman court culture which lasted from 1718 until 1730 and which was marked by intensified commercial and cultural contact with Western Europe, particularly France. Such contact was facilitated by the period of relative peace following the Treaty of Passarowitz; the court during these years was dominated by a reformist "anti-war" party of whom Nevshehirli Ibrahim was the foremost representative.

During this period, Nevshehirli Ibrahim Pasha sent an envoy on a special diplomatic mission to Paris, which at the time was under the rule of Louis XV, the great "Sun King" Louis XIV having died in 1715. The envoy in question was a confirmed Francophile who is typically credited with introducing a craze for all things French into Ottoman court circles. Indeed, the Tulip Era received its name, courtesy of a late nineteenth-century Ottoman historian, from the fad among the early eighteenth-century Ottoman elite for tulips imported via the French port of Marseilles – a rather ironic reversal of the mass European importation of Ottoman tulip bulbs during the seventeenth century, which laid the ground for Holland's famous cultivation of the flower.

For its part, the French court, which since the sixteenth century had nurtured favorable relations with the Ottoman Empire as a hedge against the expansionist Habsburgs, sent quantities of luxury goods to Topkapı Palace, including table clocks, mirrors, and Louis XV furniture – the first European-style chairs and sofas to enter the palace. Mirrors crafted in the Italian city-states likewise found their way into the palace, which was now occasionally dubbed the "palace of mirrors." By the same token, French and Italian craftsmen were employed, notably to decorate the so-called "Chamber of Fruits" which Ahmed III added to the harem complex as his personal dining room. The walls of this room are covered with panels displaying realistically painted fruits in the manner of single elements from a still-life. Such a style would have been unthinkable even a few years earlier. Meanwhile, the sultan and his grand vizier commissioned pleasure pavilions along the Bosphorus and the Golden Horn. One of the most famous of these pavilions, known as the "Mirrored Lodge," still exists on the northern shore of the Golden Horn. At this same time, French and above all Italian craftsmen were being employed directly by local notables in western Anatolia to decorate their own lavish residences. French and Italian artwork and furnishings had become, in short, status symbols both at the Ottoman court and among the Ottoman provincial elite. During this period, in consequence, large numbers of European-style clocks begin to appear in the estate registers of harem eunuchs preserved in the Topkapı Palace archives.

THE *BOOK OF FESTIVALS*

In this atmosphere, Ahmed III and his grand vizier patronized a new generation of court poets. Meanwhile, the palace and the new pleasure pavilions were the scene of literary salons and lavish evening entertainments watched and, in some cases, organized by the chief eunuch and the women of the imperial harem. This milieu is captured in the *Book of Festivals* prepared for Ahmed III in 1720 by his court chronicler, with full-page illustrations by the court painter. The work documents a lavish procession of guilds held at Istanbul's hippodrome, a grassy field a few hundred meters from the palace, adjacent to the famous Blue Mosque, as well as fireworks displays and other entertainments held at the Mirrored Lodge on the Golden Horn, to commemorate the circumcision of three of Ahmed III's fourteen sons. Not since the *Book of Festivals* of 1592, prepared for Sultan Murad III, had such a work been commissioned. Quite obviously, Ahmed III meant to invite comparison of himself to Murad III, who presided over the production of some of the greatest works of Ottoman history and literature. Noticeable in the eighteenth-century *Book of Festivals* is the influence of European painting techniques, notably a rudimentary form of perspective, as well as a less intense palette of colors. European visitors are depicted as spectators in a number of scenes, as are harem women, who appear, heads covered and faces veiled, in the rear of the crowds in several miniatures.

Furthermore, both Nevshehirli Ibrahim Pasha and Beshir Agha are well represented in this *Book of Festivals*. A two-page composition shows Beshir riding in the circumcision parade with the eunuch of the Gate of Felicity, that is, the highest-ranking white eunuch, who guarded the threshold in front of the sultan's audience chamber. Beshir is a stout man, devoid of facial hair, as were all eunuchs castrated before puberty, wearing a fur-trimmed, burgundy-colored caftan over a long-sleeved white shirt, and a white headdress of the high "sugar loaf" variety popular among palace officials of the time. The threshold eunuch is similarly corpulent and wears a drab green caftan over a white shirt. Beshir Agha rides a white horse, his counterpart a black one. In point of fact, the two eunuchs complement each other visually in a manner that may reflect either the customs followed in such a procession or the conceit of the painter. The two eunuchs are surrounded by an extensive entourage that appears to include other members of the corps of white eunuchs, as well as various mercenary soldiers.

In one of the last folios of this *Book of Festivals*, the three princes are shown being led to the Circumcision Room, in a kiosk in the palace's Fourth Court, by six viziers (two holding the arms of each prince) while Beshir Agha walks in front, this time dressed in green caftan and red shirt. Another African harem eunuch is visible, wearing an orange caftan, at the side of the grand vizier, who is bowing before the sultan in the Circumcision Room. This same personage follows the sultan on horseback when the sultan arrives at the hippodrome for the official festivities; in that case, he may be an imperial companion, perhaps even el-Hajj Beshir Agha's eventual successor, the ill-fated Moralı Beshir (on whom see chapters 4 and 12). In marked contrast, no eunuchs at all are pictured in the sixteenth-century *Book of Festivals*, although they do appear, in rather generic fashion, in the official court chronicle of Süleyman I's reign, also completed late in the sixteenth century.

8

BESHIR AGHA DURING THE REIGN OF MAHMUD I

The Tulip Era and the reign of Ahmed III, as well as the grand vizierate of Nevshehirli Ibrahim Pasha, came to an abrupt end in 1730 as a result of a massive soldiery revolt. Beshir Agha, remarkably, emerged seemingly completely unscathed from this rebellion and continued as chief eunuch under Ahmed III's successor, Sultan Mahmud I (r. 1730–54). If anything, his hold over the office of grand vizier appears to have tightened. Already in his late 70s or early 80s by the time the revolt erupted, Beshir Agha spent the last sixteen years of his life ostensibly determining, even dictating, who would run the Ottoman Empire.

THE PATRONA HALIL REBELLION, 1730

The revolt that brought down Sultan Ahmed III was instigated by an Albanian naval mercenary boss known as "Patrona" Halil. By the eighteenth century, mercenary and irregular troops had become staples of the Ottoman military forces, displacing the "classical" landgrant-holding cavalry and Janissary infantry. Nowhere was their dominance more evident than in the Ottoman navy, where mercenaries of various kinds had been indispensable since the conquest of Crete from the Venetians in 1669. Following the Habsburg reconquest of Belgrade in 1718, however, and throughout the Tulip Era, these mercenaries became increasingly disgruntled as a policy of peaceful diplomatic engagement, under the guidance of the bureaucrats who dominated Ottoman statecraft, kept the Ottoman military relatively idle.

In such circumstances, soldiers not on a fixed salary from the state, and even those who were, were obliged to ply trades on the side in order to make a living. These elements resented the peaceful diplomatic and commercial exchanges with France and other European powers. The art, literature, architecture, and entertainments of those years must have seemed wasteful and affected to them. The empire's chief religious official favored a return to *jihad*, or holy war, against the Christian enemy, whether Roman Catholic Habsburg or Orthodox Russian; the latter were a source of mounting concern as Tsar Peter the Great and his immediate successors extended Russia's empire into the Transcaucasus. This position was shared by a large number of Muslim scholar-officials in the capital. The grand vizier, Nevshehirli Ibrahim Pasha, became a focus for the resentment of these elements. Ultimately, the naval mercenary boss known as Patrona (from the Italian *patron*, or "chief") Halil led a troop of mercenaries in an uprising against the palace. They demanded the deposition of the sultan and the execution of the grand vizier. Nevshehirli Ibrahim Pasha was ultimately sacrificed to this unruly mob, while Ahmed III gave up the throne to his nephew Mahmud I, son of Mustafa II.

Beshir Agha's part in the Patrona Halil rebellion, or indeed its effect on him, is difficult to determine. He does not seem to have been a direct participant, nor was he a focus of the rebels' aggression. Given the degree of his influence in the palace and the fact that he approved, if he did not select, Nevshehirli Ibrahim Pasha as grand vizier, that he seems to have come through the rebellion entirely unscathed seems curious, indeed rather suspicious. On the other hand, he was widely known as a friend of Muslim scholar-officials and a promoter of the study of the Qur'an and the traditions of the Prophet Muhammad. It is certainly conceivable that he turned a blind eye when these scholar-officials turned against Ibrahim Pasha; he may even have manipulated their opinion against the grand vizier. He was also getting on in years by this time: perhaps around 75 or even 80, although age was no guarantee against execution. In any event, the dexterity and subtlety necessary to achieve such an end while coming to no harm oneself may be difficult to appreciate. It is useful to recall, in this regard, that Beshir Agha's successor as chief eunuch was in office for only six years before being executed, ostensibly on account of the rampages of his own military slaves.

MAHMUD I (r. 1730–54)

Regardless, Beshir Agha was not on the side of Patrona Halil and his rebel forces, although he, along with other surviving palace officials, was obliged to accede to their demands in the year following the revolt. The rebels oversaw the destruction of the courtly "pleasure grounds" on the Golden Horn and the Sea of Marmara, where members of the court had indulged in open-air entertainments during the tenure of the executed Nevshehirli Ibrahim Pasha. Following a sort of counterrevolution in 1731, possibly instigated by Ibrahim Pasha's widow, however, Mahmud I's inner circle began to take measures to rein in the rebels. Beshir Agha was instrumental in this rehabilitation of the court. His influence over Mahmud is generally conceded to have been even greater than his influence over Ahmed III. He had personally overseen the education which Mahmud, while a young prince, had received in the harem.

If Beshir Agha had acquiesced in and even facilitated the grand vizierate of Nevshehirli Ibrahim Pasha, his influence on the office of grand vizier following Nevshehirli Ibrahim's execution was absolute. European observers believed that Beshir had drawn an important lesson from the Patrona rebellion and Nevshehirli Ibrahim's fate: namely, that no grand vizier should be trusted for too long a period and that it was best to change grand viziers fairly frequently. Accordingly, the first grand vizier to hold office following the rebellion served for only three years, while his three immediate successors served for one year each.

Mahmud I's military engagements

Beshir Agha's foreign policy stance had been, up to this point, rather indeterminate. He had certainly collaborated closely with Nevshehirli

Ibrahim Pasha and the peace-minded statesmen of Ahmed III's court, yet when they were deposed by more militaristic elements, Beshir was left unharmed. He continued in office and flourished under the new sultan, who was far more caught up in military campaigns than his predecessor had been.

Beshir's role in Mahmud I's military engagements was almost certainly not direct; that is to say, he was not involved in planning strategy or negotiations. Yet the part he played in promoting one former grand vizier attests to his desire to reward a balance of military and diplomatic skills while at the same time safeguarding the interests of the Holy Cities foundations, which were always at the forefront of the chief eunuch's concerns.

Mahmud's military activity resulted in part from factors beyond his direct control. The Ottomans' traditional enemy to the east, the Twelver Shi'ite Safavid Empire, had been dealt a veritable deathblow by Sunni Afghan invaders in 1722. After a decade of chaos and uncertainty, a military commander named Nadir Shah seized power from the Afghans and, claiming to rule in the name of the Safavids, launched an aggressive expansionist campaign against Ottoman territory which resulted in clashes with Ottoman forces in Iraq, what is now Iranian Azerbaijan, and the Caucasus. One Ottoman peace overture to Nadir Shah in 1739 proposed recognizing the Twelver Shi'ism practiced in Iran as a fifth Sunni legal rite (in addition to the customary four, discussed in the Introduction); the proposal, however, ultimately came to nothing.

Hekimoğlu Ali Pasha

The situation on the Habsburg and Russian fronts, in contrast, was less chaotic and volatile. Here, a mixture of battlefield prowess and skillful diplomacy yielded the most satisfying results. A signal success for the Ottomans was the recapture of Banja Luka in northern Bosnia from the Habsburgs in 1737, followed in 1739 by a treaty which resulted in the return of Belgrade and surrounding territories to Ottoman control and won the Ottomans forty years of peace on their western border. The reconqueror of Banja Luka and one of the architects of the peace was the first post-Patrona Halil grand vizier, Hekimoğlu ("son of the doctor") Ali Pasha, who had just returned from a five-year exile on Crete. Beshir Agha was almost certainly instrumental in Hekimoğlu Ali's appointment as grand vizier, exile, and recall to active service.

After his signal military and diplomatic victories in the Balkans, Hekimoğlu Ali Pasha went on to Cairo, where he served as governor of Egypt for two years (1739–41) before being recalled to the grand vizierate for six months during 1742. He was eventually reappointed to Egypt in 1754, some eight years after Beshir Agha's death, and served for two years.

Hekimoğlu Ali's two postings to Egypt are especially telling in view of Beshir Agha's concerns regarding the collection of revenues for the pious foundations of the Holy Cities. A contemporary Egyptian chronicler attributes Hekimoğlu Ali's initial appointment as Egyptian governor to a dream he had while encamped below the walls of Banja Luka in 1737: the founders of four Egyptian mystical orders appeared to him and promised that, if he agreed to go to Egypt, he would recapture the city. The same chronicler claims that on his installation in Cairo's citadel in 1739, only months after the critical treaty with the Habsburgs was signed, Hekimoğlu Ali announced to Cairo's assembled grandees that he was not there to quell a revolt or to kill people but simply to ensure the delivery of the revenues that Egypt owed, above all to the Holy Cities endowments. His rhetoric must have had great resonance, given the fact that only three years earlier, the major provincial supervisors of the Holy Cities foundations – who were, not coincidentally, Egypt's leading military officers and subprovincial governors – had been assassinated at the behest of the then-governor. This act allowed the imperial treasury to confiscate the estates of a number of the deceased while naming new figures to the helms of the pious foundations.

Such tactics were common during the 1730s and 1740s, when the leaders of the Qazdağlı household, seeking to consolidate their hold on Egypt's major revenue sources, not infrequently withheld revenues from the imperial treasury and from the Holy Cities. As noted in chapter 6, the Qazdağlı household had been founded by the regimental officer who dominated Egypt in conjunction with Beshir Agha's putative patron, Ismail Bey, in the late seventeenth century. The household dominated Egypt's Janissary regiment in the early years of the eighteenth century and, by the 1730s, was poised to become the most influential household in Egypt. The assassination schemes, however, led to a messy situation in which the Ottoman governor seemed to be joining in the struggle for revenues and positions between the Qazdağlıs and the households which sought to counter them. Hekimoğlu Ali Pasha, at least so far as the chronicler was concerned, transcended such partisan conflicts.

By 1754, the rival households had been vanquished, and Qazdağlı control over Egypt was all but absolute. When Hekimoğlu Ali Pasha arrived in Cairo for a second term, then, he confronted a new reality. Yet in the aforementioned Egyptian chronicle, the triumphant accession scene is repeated. So far as the chronicler was concerned, Hekimoğlu Ali was associated with a properly functioning provincial government that remitted the revenues required of it to the Holy Cities. His two appointments as governor of Egypt clearly reflect the agenda of Beshir Agha and of Beshir Agha's immediate successor.

Hekimoğlu Ali Pasha's experience is only the most graphic illustration of Beshir Agha's thorough-going political influence during the reign of Mahmud I. His successor as grand vizier, a much less adept statesman who was reportedly illiterate, was utterly ruined by Beshir Agha's death in 1746. Not only did the elderly eunuch control the grand vizierate; he manipulated current and former occupants of that office so as to pursue his agenda vis-à-vis Egypt and the Holy Cities. At the same time, he cannot be accused of tunnel vision, focusing obsessively on the Holy Cities endowments, although these were the chief eunuch's prime concern. His promotion of Hekimoğlu Ali Pasha demonstrates a broader vision of the Ottoman Empire's geopolitical interests. In the geopolitical arena, he made concessions to the more militarized conditions of Mahmud I's reign while still pursuing the diplomatic agenda of Ahmed III's old "peace party" where possible.

9

BESHIR AGHA AND THE ARAB PROVINCES

THE PILGRIMAGE CARAVAN AND THE GOVERNORSHIP OF DAMASCUS

The first half of the eighteenth century was a time when services to the Holy Cities, along with command of the pilgrimage caravan, were becoming tendentious issues in the Ottoman Empire's Arab provinces, and above all in the key provincial capitals of Cairo and Damascus. Each city sent an annual pilgrimage caravan to Mecca and Medina. In 1708, the governor of Damascus began to serve as commander of the Damascus pilgrimage caravan, meaning that he now spent much of the year either traveling with the caravan or overseeing its provisioning and preparing for its departure. His deputy, who remained behind in Damascus to administer the province in the governor's absence, now assumed unusually great importance. On the other hand, the new duties meant that the governor became a highly visible exponent of Ottoman authority throughout the province of Damascus, which encompassed not only the bulk of modern-day Syria but also Lebanon, Palestine, and the region of what is now Jordan.

The Azms

Between 1720 and 1770, the governorship of Damascus, along with the subordinate governorships of Tripoli and Sidon in Lebanon and the governorship of Aleppo in northern Syria, was dominated by one provincial notable family, the Azms. This was an Arab, Sunni Muslim family with deep roots in Damascus and vicinity. They were evidently already entrenched in the region, serving as administrators for the Mamluk sultanate, when the Ottomans conquered Syria in 1516. One of them entered Ottoman military service in the seventeenth century and was awarded a grant of land-tax revenues in exchange for battlefield duty. Later generations rose farther through the chain of military-administrative command and began to acquire governorships in the 1720s. The Azm governors were thoroughly familiar with the region, and also cultivated ties with the Turcoman and bedouin tribes along the pilgrimage route who might have threatened the caravan.

The Azms could not have held these governorships without the acquiescence, or at least tolerance, of Beshir Agha. This they evidently managed to secure with one major exception during the last ten years of his tenure. During this period, Beshir Agha threw his support behind a rival notable of Damascus: one Fathi Efendi, the grandson of a weaver from western Syria. Fathi's father had become chief financial administrator of the entire province of Damascus. Fathi himself obtained the same post in 1736; indeed, his title, *Efendi*, indicates a member of the Ottoman scribal bureaucracy. He used his new office to launch a campaign to displace the Azms. The death of one of the Azm governors in 1743 gave Fathi the opportunity, as chief financial officer, to confiscate his estate. This was standard Ottoman governmental practice on the death of an official, yet the zeal with which Fathi went about it angered the remaining Azms and their supporters. When another Azm was appointed to succeed the deceased governor, Fathi began ever more blatantly to maneuver to bring down the successor and assume the governorship himself. His efforts were cut short by Beshir Agha's death in 1746, which enabled the Azm governor to use his own connections in Istanbul to secure Fathi's execution for corrupt practices.

In the years following Beshir's death, an episode occurred that presumably caused high officials in the palace to realize just how valuable the Azms were in ensuring the security of the pilgrimage caravan. In 1757, a figure named Husayn ibn al-Makki ("son of the

Meccan") used his influence with the then chief harem eunuch, Ebukoff Ahmed Agha, to secure the governorship of Damascus for himself. He did not, however, enjoy the ties to the regional tribes that the Azms had carefully cultivated. In consequence, the caravan that he set out to lead in 1757 was attacked by bedouins in the western Arabian peninsula and pillaged; hundreds of pilgrims were killed, others taken captive. Ibn al-Makki managed to escape and make his way back to Damascus, but he was in disgrace and was deposed the following year. His successor was a Georgian former mamluk, or elite slave, of a former Azm governor.

Syria versus Egypt

The administrative change whereby the governor of Damascus assumed the responsibilities of pilgrimage caravan leader made the Syrian caravan that much more visible and distinctive en route to and in the Holy Cities. Moreover, since the governor now led the caravan in person, departure and arrival ceremonies became larger and more grandiose, features that prompted a rivalry with the Egyptian caravan, which was still led by a subprovincial governor holding the rank of *bey*. Competition between the Damascene and Egyptian pilgrimage commanders would culminate in the 1760s, when Ali Bey, commander of the Egyptian pilgrimage caravan, blatantly sought to upstage the Damascus caravan, led by the aforementioned former mamluk of the Azms. Ali Bey was unable to secure the governorship of Egypt through recognized channels, in marked contrast to his Syrian counterpart, who, although the locally trained mamluk of the Azm family, was nonetheless installed by the Ottoman central authority as governor of the province of Damascus. This career frustration may have been partially responsible for Ali Bey's all-out rebellion against the Ottoman sultan in 1768. Likewise, it may have factored to some degree in the continual suspense, during Beshir Agha's tenure, as to whether one or another Egyptian grandee would rebel against Istanbul. During the 1720s, the Venetian ambassador strongly suspected that one of two rival leaders of the Qasimi faction would uncouple Egypt from the Ottoman domains.

BESHIR AGHA AND EGYPT'S GRANDEES

Ismail Bey son of Ivaz Bey

Although Beshir Agha did not habitually support members of the Qasimi faction – as opposed to the rival Faqari faction – in Egypt, he seems to have supported one Qasimi leader, however grudgingly, during the 1720s. The early 1720s were a rather anomalous period in Egypt, when two rival branches of the Qasimi faction vied for control of the villages endowed to the pious foundations for the Holy Cities with relatively little interference from the Faqari faction. (This may have been because, in the wake of the 1711 "civil war," described in chapter 5, Faqari influence was concentrated in the Janissary regiment rather than in the subprovincial governorships that carried the rank of *bey*; the subprovincial governors had far more direct access to villages, endowed or otherwise, than Janissary officers.) Beshir Agha was thus obliged to choose between the two rival Qasimi branches, which were headed by Ismail Bey son of Ivaz Bey and by one Cherkes Mehmed Bey, whose nickname, Cherkes, referred to his origins in the region of the Caucasus Mountains known as Circassia (today part of southern Russia). Beshir appears to have given his support to Ismail Bey for reasons that remain unclear but that may have had something to do with the chief eunuch's far more direct connection to a different household in Egypt.

The Jalfi household

This household, known as the Jalfi household, would come to dominate Egypt's Azeban regiment, the second largest of Egypt's seven regiments of soldiery after the Janissaries, and would serve as a partner to the Qazdağlı household, which, as noted in chapters 6 and 8, became a force in Egyptian politics early in the eighteenth century. The Jalfi household came into existence when one of Beshir Agha's mamluks, Mehmed, who seems to have been a commanding officer of the Azeban, married his own mamluk, Hasan, a slightly lower-ranking regimental officer, to the daughter of a notable from the Nile Delta village of Sanjalf, whence comes the adjective Jalfi. (Village names derived from the ancient language of Egypt's Coptic Christians frequently contained the prefix *san-* or *sand-*, an equivalent of "Saint" which was often omitted from adjectival forms of the name.) Beshir Agha's mamluk Mehmed may originally have been a member of one of the corps of soldiery connected with the imperial palace in Istanbul; such elite troops from the imperial capital were not infrequently appointed commanders of Egypt's regiments until early in the eighteenth century. Mehmed was probably already established in Egypt before Beshir's temporary exile there in 1713 or so, to judge from a plausible reference to his own mamluk, Hasan, in an archival document in 1711.

In 1712, the year of his death, Hasan settled a dispute over an Upper Egyptian village endowed to the Holy Cities between Ismail Bey son of Ivaz and a Faqari grandee. Ismail Bey was about to seize the village from the Faqari when Hasan al-Jalfi intervened and forced the two to agree to share the village's revenues equally for the duration of Hasan's lifetime. Ismail Bey clearly agreed to the settlement out of respect for (and perhaps fear of) Hasan's authority, to say nothing of the armed might at his disposal.

Hasan al-Jalfi would in turn acquire a mamluk called Ali who would surpass him as a household-builder and leader of the Azeban regiment. While still a lower-ranking officer in the Azeban corps, Ali served his patron as treasurer in a rather striking parallel to the prevalent career path for chief harem eunuchs, whereby the harem treasurer succeeded to the post of chief eunuch. Ali was murdered in 1738 at the instigation of Egypt's governor, who, rather ironically, was the only member of the Azm dynasty ever to govern Egypt, as opposed to one of the Syrian provinces or districts. His murder was part of a larger plot, typical of Ottoman governors of Egypt during this period, to eliminate the holders of Egypt's top administrative positions so as to acquire their wealth for the imperial treasury.

Notwithstanding, Ali's murder did not put an end to Jalfi influence, for his mamluk Rıdvan assumed control of the Azeban regiment and forged a full-fledged partnership with the then-leader of the Qazdağlı household, Ibrahim, who dominated the Janissary corps. This partnership was largely commercial, as opposed to military: Rıdvan al-Jalfi received one-third of the profits from the trade in Yemeni coffee that came into Ibrahim's hands by virtue of Qazdağlı control of port customs and their own direct investments in the coffee trade.

With this wealth, Rıdvan al-Jalfi built a large mansion on the shores of the Azbakiyya pond, the new hub of elite residence in what was then the northwest of Cairo, and sponsored a literary salon, as well as night-time entertainments on the banks of the pond. The period of Rıdvan's efflorescence, roughly 1748–54, marks the height of this brand of elite culture, which must have resembled in some respects a latter-day Tulip Era. Following the death of his partner Ibrahim al-Qazdağlı in 1754, however, Rıdvan was attacked and killed by the son of an earlier Qazdağlı leader whom Ibrahim had protected. After this, the Jalfi household existed as a decidedly subordinate household to the Qazdağlıs until the late eighteenth century.

Rıdvan al-Jalfi's cultural patronage cannot, of course, be attributed to his household's historical links with Beshir Agha. However, the Jalfi household's peculiar role in Egypt's political culture may have had something to do with its links to the chief harem eunuch. Historically, although chief harem eunuchs had acquired mamluks and other clients in Egypt, these clients had never been able to build highly influential, self-sustaining households. Even Yusuf Agha, the chief harem eunuch who, as noted in chapter 4, was by far the most active in Egyptian politics following his exile to Cairo in 1687, left behind very few prominent clients following his death sometime around 1700. In this respect, Beshir was unprecedented among chief harem eunuchs, exiled or otherwise, in actually founding, albeit indirectly, a household that not only survived for three-quarters of a century but that took a central role in Egypt's economy, political culture, and cultural life.

On the other hand, the Jalfi household seems always to have played a subordinate role to another household, above all to the Qazdağlıs. Furthermore, the mediating role assumed by successive Jalfi leaders is striking. Hasan, Ali, and Rıdvan in turn intervened to resolve disputes over the tax farms of Upper Egyptian towns and villages during the first half of the eighteenth century. Although not all these locales were endowed to the Holy Cities pious foundations, the Jalfis may have undertaken to safeguard the status of endowed towns and villages by way of ensuring that their revenues actually went toward the upkeep of Mecca and Medina.

Effects of Beshir Agha's death in Egypt

Beshir Agha's death in 1746 does not appear to have had a direct effect on the Jalfi household. It did, however, have rather dire ramifications for two other Egyptian households: the Dumyatis, Faqari allies who controlled the customs at the Mediterranean port of Damietta (Dumyat in Arabic), and the Qatamish household, which formed within the Faqari faction during the late 1710s and which by the 1740s had emerged as a potential rival to the Qazdağlıs.

Since Beshir Agha had no heirs, those portions of his estate which were not endowed as pious foundations could be confiscated by the imperial treasury. This fact set off a wave of confiscation attempts throughout the empire, for Beshir Agha had clients and properties in virtually every province. In Egypt, his agent, or *wakil*, Osman Agha, attempted to reclaim left-over grain and revenues from the villages endowed to the Holy Cities foundations. These were in the possession of two leaders of the Qatamish household and a Dumyati ally of theirs who acted as financial administrator of Egypt. (In one tense moment captured – or invented – by an Egyptian chronicler, Osman Agha pointedly asked Ibrahim Bey Qatamish what the rebellious cavalry troops would eat if Ibrahim did not release the grain. Ibrahim allegedly retorted, "The soldiers can eat my shit!" Damurdashi *c.*1755, p. 528.) The obstinate refusal of the Qatamish and Dumyati grandees to relinquish the grain led the Ottoman governor to request an imperial order authorizing him to assassinate the Qatamish leadership and exile the remaining Dumyatis from Egypt. These actions eliminated the Qatamish and Dumyati households as political forces in Egypt. In short, two major Egyptian households were eclipsed as an indirect result of the death in far-away Istanbul of the chief harem eunuch.

Osman Agha, the "agent of the harem"

Osman Agha is certainly the best-documented of Beshir Agha's and possibly of any chief harem eunuch's *wakil*s, or agents. It becomes clear from references to him in Egyptian chronicles and from archival records concerning his activities in Egypt that Osman Agha was Beshir's permanent representative in Egypt, and that this office was probably institutionalized, although when it became an institution is unclear. In other words, there was always an "agent of the harem" resident in Cairo to oversee the acting chief eunuch's affairs, as well as the business of the Holy Cities endowments. This official no doubt dealt with former chief eunuchs resident in Cairo as well. His residence was probably in the same neighborhood as that of the exiled chief eunuchs: around the pond known as Birkat al-Fil, west of Cairo's citadel, during the late seventeenth and early eighteenth centuries, and around the Azbakiyya pond later in the eighteenth century. Osman's residence was probably at Azbakiyya, near the houses of the Qazdağlı leaders of the time, as well as that of a later Beshir Agha. Indeed, Osman may have been responsible for securing a house at Azbakiyya for el-Hajj Beshir, who probably expected to be exiled to Cairo at some point, not realizing that he would be one of the few chief eunuchs to die in office.

As to Osman Agha's identity, he appears to have been, like the earlier *wakil* Hasan Agha, discussed in chapter 5, a commanding officer of one of Egypt's military regiments. One provincial chronicle gives a considerable amount of information about him. Known in Arabic as "short," and later as "father of the sword," a military honorific, he appears to have been a client of Ibrahim al-Qazdağlı, the partner of Rıdvan al-Jalfi, who was the most powerful of Egypt's grandees during the 1740s. At Ibrahim's instigation, the governor of Egypt at the time made Osman commander (*agha*) of the regiment of soldiery most closely connected with the governor's council. Shortly thereafter, Ibrahim al-Qazdağlı promoted Osman to *bey* and made him governor of the grain-rich superprovince of Jirja in Upper Egypt, a key source of the grain delivered to the Holy Cities by the Egyptian pilgrimage caravan each year. To acquire this post, Osman Agha had to kill the previous occupant, a member of the above-mentioned Qatamish household, which he did as part of a campaign by Ibrahim al-Qazdağlı, with the governor's approval, against the entire Qatamish household.

As noted in chapter 5, the *wakil* appears most frequently as a commercial agent who handles sales and purchases for his employer. Osman Agha's duties would appear to fall preponderantly in this category, although he no doubt represented Beshir Agha in the Muslim law courts as well. One critical feature of his work was that while Beshir Agha was acting chief harem eunuch, and therefore based in Istanbul, Osman Agha acted with relative independence in Cairo. In that respect, he was Beshir's agent in a very broad sense, almost as if he were an administrative deputy. He had the authority not only to purchase a house or slaves, or to commission a fountain, but to intervene in the provincial administration of the Holy Cities endowment revenues, as we see above in his alleged confrontation with Ibrahim Bey Qatamish.

An agent such as Osman Agha would, in addition, have had to have the interests of the Holy Cities pious foundations at the forefront of his conscience. Certainly the "agent of the harem" was appointed first and foremost to ensure that the revenues and grains endowed to the Holy Cities were collected and delivered to Cairo, and that they then made their way to Mecca and Medina with the annual pilgrimage caravan. He therefore had to have an intimate knowledge of Egypt's grandees, including the pilgrimage commander; holders of subprovincial tax farms, particularly those of the grain-rich districts of Upper Egypt; and Janissaries who guarded the pilgrimage route. He would also have been familiar with the various bedouin chieftains along the route, and may have been instrumental in ensuring that they received the gifts, including robes of honor, that encouraged them to protect, rather than attack, the pilgrim caravan. In the Arabian peninsula, meanwhile, he would have been acquainted with the *sharif*, or descendant of the Prophet Muhammad, who administered Mecca on behalf of the Ottomans and, naturally, with the eunuchs who guarded the Prophet's tomb in Medina and their chief.

Ultimately, of course, it fell to the agent's lot to pick up what pieces he could of Beshir Agha's estate once the elderly eunuch had died. In the absence of heirs, this typically meant a lengthy rendering of accounts, above all accounting for the revenues and grains owed to the pious foundations of the Holy Cities. This sort of task could take years and undoubtedly represented the "agent of the harem's" most tedious and time-consuming chore.

10

BESHIR AGHA'S LIBRARIES AND PIOUS FOUNDATIONS

We cannot conclude the discussion of Beshir Agha's life without acknowledging the many educational and religious foundations which he established in the course of his lengthy career. These take the form of several substantial libraries in Istanbul and in the Arab provinces, as well as numerous mosques, theological colleges, and fountains throughout the Ottoman Empire. These undertakings not only attest to the widespread influence of the man who launched them; they provide critical clues to his intellectual preferences and religious leanings and, beyond these, to his sense of himself as an Ottoman who promoted and helped to shape the religious and cultural agenda of the Ottoman central authority.

LIBRARIES

Beshir Agha's own tastes and proclivities surely influenced intellectual production at the courts of Sultans Ahmed III and Mahmud I. Like many chief eunuchs, he collected large numbers of books on a variety of topics. The starting point for such a collection was the curriculum of the palace school, in which the eunuchs were educated and whose operation the white eunuchs ultimately oversaw. Central to the palace school curriculum were Islamic law and theology according to the Hanafi legal rite, which, as noted in the Introduction, the Ottomans promoted as their official rite, as well as Persian poetry and the canonical narrative of Ottoman history as embodied in the *History of the Ottoman Dynasty*. Palace functionaries trained in this school thus became an intellectual as well as a status elite.

Ottoman palace eunuchs, like court eunuchs in many empires, felt that they had a personal stake in the cultivation and preservation of high court culture. Perhaps for this reason, many of them became book-collectors and -fanciers. Those eunuchs who were exiled to Cairo carried their libraries with them. An estate inventory of the late seventeenth-century chief eunuch Abbas Agha (tenure 1667–71), who died in Cairo in the late 1600s, includes a list of twenty-four books ranging from classics of Hanafi theology, composed in medieval Central Asia, through the *History of the Ottoman Dynasty* and classic collections of Persian poetry to a work on medicine, collections of sufi (mystical) prayers, and biographies of sufi adepts. Abbas Agha also collected precious illuminated Qur'an manuscripts; indeed, his Qur'an collection appears to have been rather well known to Cairo's cognoscenti. Thus, an imperial order of 1697 demands that the governor of Egypt cease his attempts to confiscate the manuscript collection. Under Hanafi law, it was possible to endow collections of books as pious foundations; hence the attraction of investing in costly manuscripts.

The reign of Ahmed III was, furthermore, a period in which libraries became a focus of palace attention. In 1719, the sultan himself founded a new library in the Third Court of Topkapı Palace, just behind the sultan's audience chamber and only a few meters away from the current palace library. (There is some speculation that the idea for this library may have come from Beshir Agha.) The period of cultural efflorescence and European cultural contact known as the Tulip Era (1718–30), discussed in chapter 7, saw the introduction of the printing press in Ottoman territories and the consequent printing of a number of works of Muslim law and theology, as well as the chronicle of the first official Ottoman court historian. Greater contact with Europe also encouraged the acquisition by the sultan and his grand vizier of European manuscripts and printed books, as well as the composition of new collections of poetry and, as noted in chapter 7, a new *Book of Festivals*. Numerous sixteenth-century treatises and chronicles were recopied in the eighteenth century, indicating a renewed interest in these works on the part of Ottoman officialdom. The new prominence of what the historian Norman Itzkowitz calls "efendis-turned-pashas" (Itzkowitz 1962, p. 81) – that is, viziers and other high officials who came from the ranks of the Ottoman bureaucracy rather than from military backgrounds – may have played a part in this apparent wave of bibliophilia.

Beshir Agha, for his part, was clearly one of the great bibliophiles of the eighteenth century. There is no reason to believe that his interest in books – or that of any other chief eunuch, for that matter – was merely financial, rather than intellectual, in nature. The French merchant Jean-Claude Flachat, who became a close associate of el-Hajj Beshir Agha's successor, Moralı Beshir Agha (tenure 1746–52), reports that Moralı Beshir spent many hours each day reading in his library. El-Hajj Beshir, under whose supervision Moralı Beshir had served as harem treasurer, undoubtedly had similar tastes. His own collection, like that of the seventeenth-century chief eunuch Abbas Agha, was rich in works of Hanafi law and theology, as well as works of history and literature in Ottoman Turkish, Persian, and Arabic.

To the right of the prayer hall in the mosque that Beshir Agha commissioned near Topkapı Palace (to be discussed below) is a long, narrow room that apparently housed at least part of his library. A separate structure was founded in 1735 in the quarter of Eyüp outside Istanbul's Byzantine land walls, site of the city's largest cemetery, where Beshir Agha and many other prominent Ottoman officials are buried. This smaller collection consisted mainly of theological works, doubtless Hanafi for the most part. In 1743, it was enriched by the addition of the books that Ahmed III's mother, Gülnush Emetullah, had endowed to the library of Istanbul's famous Ayasofya (Hagia Sophia) mosque. Today, the books from both these collections which remained in the capital after the declaration of the Turkish Republic are housed in two special classifications in the Süleymaniye Library: classification Beshir Agha, comprising the books held in the mosque library, and classification Beshir Agha Eyüp, comprising the books held in the library at Eyüp.

HOLDINGS OF BESHIR AGHA'S LIBRARY OUTSIDE THE PALACE

A catalogue of the books collected in the room adjoining the prayer hall of Beshir Agha's mosque near the palace was published in Ottoman Turkish in 1885. Most of the 690 works (in 1007 volumes, counting duplicate copies and multi-volume works) listed were presumably collected personally by Beshir and stored in this small room, which, frankly, does not appear capable of holding so many books – that is, if they are placed in vertical rows on shelves, according to standard library arrangement. It may be, however, that this room functioned as a sort of book depot from which books could be requested, then fetched by a knowledgeable librarian or mosque attendant, much as they are today in Istanbul's manuscript libraries. This could, furthermore, explain why the books were stored right next to the mosque's prayer room: valuable belongings were arguably safest in a sacred precinct of this sort. This, after all, was why the central treasury of the Umayyad caliphs in the eighth century was located in the courtyard of the Great Mosque in Damascus, and why the treasury of the Prophet Muhammad's mosque in Medina was located in the vestibule leading directly to his cenotaph, where only tomb eunuchs were allowed to go.

Although a few of the 1007 volumes listed in the nineteenth-century inventory may have been added after Beshir Agha's death, the bulk of them were his personal choices, which give us a sense of his intellectual formation and proclivities. The late Ottoman officials who prepared the printed catalogue divided the books into twenty categories, starting with four Qur'ans and continuing:

- Qur'anic exegesis: 75 volumes
- sayings of the Prophet Muhammad: 105 volumes
- Islamic jurisprudence: 21 volumes
- Islamic law: 105 volumes
- legal opinions: 26 volumes
- sufism (Islamic mysticism): 48 volumes
- theology: 30 volumes

- wisdom literature/aphorisms: 6 volumes
- logic: 4 volumes
- astronomy/astrology and prognostication: 19 volumes
- history: 58 volumes
- medicine: 20 volumes
- "literature" (including poetry): 35 volumes
- "investigation and examination" (rhetoric): 25 volumes
- grammar: 32 volumes
- morphology: 7 volumes
- language: 30 volumes
- miscellaneous collections: 33 volumes
- miscellaneous treatises: 324 volumes.

The nineteenth-century scribes also noted the physical appearance of the volumes, most of which were embellished with subheadings in gold leaf, costly leather bindings, and so on. Obviously, Beshir Agha was a collector of rare, costly specimens; however, he also cultivated interests in a wide variety of subjects.

Islamic law and theology

In marked contrast to the library of the seventeenth-century eunuch Abbas Agha, Beshir's contains only four Qur'an manuscripts. There were doubtless originally many more, but these may have been among the books he bequeathed to al-Azhar university in Cairo (noted below), which must have been in continual need of Qur'an manuscripts for its many students. Otherwise, his library parallels that of Abbas Agha in its collection of canonical works of Qur'anic exegesis, law, and theology according to the Hanafi legal rite of Sunni Islam, which, as noted in the Introduction, was the official Ottoman rite. These works included numerous classics of the genre composed in medieval Central Asia. However, Beshir Agha's collection shows a keen awareness of theological developments in the seventeenth century. He seems to have owned a few key texts associated with the puritanical, anti-sufi religious tendency known as the Kadızadeli movement, which was influential in Istanbul between the 1630s and the 1680s. His library contains several copies of the *Treatise* of a sixteenth-century judge from a provincial town in western Anatolia; this work was considered a prooftext of the Kadızadelis. In addition, he owned a work of Qur'anic exegesis by a student of Sultan Mehmed IV's spiritual adviser, who led the Kadızadeli movement during the 1660s and 1670s; this later Kadızadeli leader persuaded the Jewish messianic figure Sabbatai Sevi to convert to Islam in 1666. Especially numerous among Beshir's exegetical works are those of the thirteenth-century Iranian judge and exegete popularly known as Qadi Baydawi, whose digest of Qur'anic exegesis was extraordinarily influential in the Ottoman Empire. Among collections of *hadith*, or sayings of the Prophet Muhammad, Ottoman-era compilations by well-known Egyptian jurists of both the Hanafi and Shafi'i legal rites are numerous. Legal decisions of jurists active in various Ottoman provinces during the later decades of the seventeenth century are collected here as well.

Sufism

Like Abbas Agha, and despite his ownership of Kadızadeli works, Beshir Agha appears to have had a strong interest in Islamic mysticism, or sufism, illustrated by his possession of numerous mystical works of the great eleventh-century Sunni theologian al-Ghazali (d. 1111) and of the controversial Spanish mystic Ibn Arabi (d. 1240), whose doctrine that God is present in all of creation led some orthodox theologians to accuse him of pantheism. Also represented in his collection are the works of famous Arab and Persian mystics of the Middle Ages, including two manuscripts of the lengthy Persian mystical poem composed by Mevlana Jalal al-Din Rumi (d. 1273), founder of the so-called "whirling dervishes." The collection also boasts mystical poetry and treatises by well-known Ottoman-era mystics, composed in both Ottoman Turkish and Arabic. Notable is the presence of works by mystical adepts of a variety of sufi orders, indicating a general interest in mysticism on Beshir Agha's part, despite his apparent preference for one particular order, noted below.

Sciences

In striking contrast to the wealth of books in the religious sciences and sufism in Beshir's collection is the decidedly modest representation of the rational and natural sciences. The nineteenth-century printed catalogue of his library lists an Arabic translation of "The Eight Books of Aristotle," which may be a standard collection of Aristotelian works. These are joined by a fifteenth-century Central Asian astronomical almanac, a geographical work by a famous thirteenth-century Iranian philosopher, and several works on astrology, which was of great importance in most premodern royal courts. Books on fortune-telling and amulets indicate a complementary interest in more down-to-earth forms of "folk" science.

Like Abbas Agha's library, on the other hand, Beshir's contained a fairly substantial number of medical works, indicating that it may have been the norm for chief eunuchs to be concerned with medicine, possibly because of the various ailments to which eunuchs were subject as they aged. Beshir's collection is notable for several manuscripts of the *Canon* of medicine, composed by the famous medieval Muslim philosopher Avicenna (Ibn Sina, d. 1037), along with numerous commentaries thereon; this work was in use even in Western Europe until well into the nineteenth century.

History

Beshir Agha's collection of history books or, more properly, annals, shows him to have kept abreast of Ottoman historical writing and works in related genres. Remarkably, he owned all ten volumes of the travelogue of the peripatetic seventeenth-century courtier Evliya Chelebi, who had died in Cairo only in 1682 or thereabouts; the Beshir Agha manuscripts comprise one of only three complete sets extant today. There is, in fact, some speculation among scholars that it was Beshir who first brought Evliya Chelebi's work to Istanbul. These manuscripts were copied in 1745, indicating that Beshir may have commissioned the copies himself shortly before his death. He also owned the version of the *History of the Ottoman Dynasty* composed by the official court historian active in the mid-seventeenth century, as well as that author's biography of the Prophet Muhammad, and the work of naval history by the seventeenth-century polymath Katib Chelebi (d. 1657).

Familiarity with medieval Iranian history and letters is indicated by a manuscript of the epic of the pre-Islamic Iranian kings, penned in the tenth century, as well as a well-known eleventh-century history of the rulers of what are now eastern Iran and northwestern Afghanistan. The history of the Mamluk sultanate, which ruled Egypt, Syria, and the Holy Cities of Mecca and Medina before the Ottoman conquest in 1517, is represented by the writings of several famous Mamluk-era chroniclers. Meanwhile, a treatise "on the Beginnings of the Circassian State" also evinces interest in the period, beginning in the late fourteenth century, when the Mamluk sultanate was dominated by rulers originally from the region of Circassia in the Caucasus Mountains. The chief harem eunuch's unique relationship to the Holy Cities of Mecca and Medina is illustrated by several works on those two cities, on the pilgrimage to Mecca, on the pilgrimage ritual of circumambulating the Ka'ba, on the birth of the Prophet Muhammad, and on visiting the tombs of the Prophet and his family in Medina. These are joined by an intriguing Arabic history of the ceremonial covering for the Ka'ba by one Mehmed Agha, a former chief of the eunuchs who guarded the Prophet Muhammad's tomb in Medina.

"Literature" and language

The broad category of "literature" includes the œuvres of several legendary medieval Persian poets and the above-mentioned Ottoman polymath Katib Chelebi's *Balance of Truth*, a short treatise covering various religious topics of moment in seventeenth-century Istanbul, including the confrontation between the Kadızadelis and the leaders of an influential sufi order. The numerous books on grammar and language, many in Arabic, suggest that Beshir Agha revered the Arabic language as the language of the Qur'an and the Prophet Muhammad, and had put some effort into mastering it.

Miscellaneous

Peculiar tidbits represented in Beshir Agha's library include a work on dream interpretation, comparable to one in the seventeenth-century eunuch Abbas Agha's collection. Two treatises speak to the cultural encounter between the Ottoman central lands, particularly the imperial capital, and Egypt, where the chief harem eunuch typically started his career and where he frequently finished it, as well. One, entitled "On the Imitation of the Shafi'is by the Hanafis," alludes to the historical rivalry between the Shafi'i and Hanafi legal rites of Sunni Islam. In medieval Iran, the two rites coalesced into opposing factions whose conflicts laid entire cities waste. By the Ottoman period, the intensity of the antagonism was much reduced; still, given that Hanafism was the official Ottoman rite, tension with Shafi'i jurists was all but inevitable in Egypt, where the Shafi'i rite had historically dominated but where the Hanafi rite was only lightly represented.

Another treatise, entitled "An Explanation of the False Rites, such as [those of] the Shi'ites," may possibly reflect ongoing tensions with Iran, even after the Shi'ite Safavid dynasty had succumbed to Sunni Afghan invaders in 1722. As noted in chapter 8, a military commander named Nadir Shah had seized power from the Afghans during the 1730s and, claiming to rule in the name of the Safavids, launched an expansionist campaign against Ottoman territory. One Ottoman peace overture to Nadir Shah in 1739 proposed recognizing the Twelver Shi'ism practiced in Iran as a fifth Sunni legal rite.

There is also a treatise on "The Laws of Smoking," perhaps in defense of that widespread practice – one in which harem eunuchs are known to have indulged – which had come under attack by none other than the envoy whom grand vizier Nevshehirli Ibrahim Pasha had sent to France at the beginning of the Tulip Era.

A new eighteenth-century curriculum?

Beshir Agha's eclectic collection gives important clues to the intellectual formation of palace eunuchs, and by extension all palace officials, in the early eighteenth century. The curriculum undergirding this formation built on the "classical" Ottoman palace curriculum, featuring seminal works of Hanafi jurisprudence composed in medieval Central Asia, classic collections of medieval Persian poetry, and early versions of the *History of the Ottoman Dynasty*, and added far more recent theological and historical works, including treatments of some of the seventeenth century's most hotly contested religious controversies. While the keen interest in libraries and book-collecting that we observe among early eighteenth-century Ottoman officials may not by itself be proof of intellectual vigor, their attention to recent and contemporary theological debates militates against the conventional argument that Ottoman intellectual life, particularly after the sixteenth century, was stagnant. Meanwhile, the breadth and variety of post-sixteenth-century compositions to be found in such libraries attest to the productivity of Ottoman theologians, intellectuals, and litterateurs during this period, and the engagement of many of these works with distinctly Ottoman-era issues calls into question the standard claim that post-sixteenth-century Ottoman intellectual output was unoriginal and derivative.

Distinctive to the collections of imperial harem eunuchs such as Beshir Agha, meanwhile, were works that addressed the interface between the imperial capital and the Holy Cities of Mecca and Medina, as well as the encounter between the Hanafi legal rite, which predominated in Istanbul, and the Shafi'i rite prevalent in Egypt. In many respects, Beshir's library reflects a hybrid intellectual formation influenced by his experiences in both the Ottoman imperial capital and the Ottoman Arab provinces.

OTHER LIBRARIES

Not all of Beshir Agha's books remained in Istanbul. He founded a library, chiefly of theological works, at Medina, endowed a pious foundation of books in Baghdad – which, only a few years before, had narrowly escaped capture by the Safavid revivalist Nadir Shah – and also bequeathed a portion of his immense book collection to the residential college of the Turks at al-Azhar university in Cairo. When we recall that religious and legal education in Ottoman Cairo, as in any Ottoman city during the eighteenth century (despite the recent introduction of the printing press), was dependent on handwritten manuscripts, we can begin to appreciate the significance of this bequest. Those colleges of al-Azhar that followed the Hanafi legal rite must have been in constant need of fresh copies of the Hanafi classics, most of which would have been produced outside of Egypt. Beshir Agha, along with the many harem eunuchs exiled to Cairo, must have provided a fairly reliable supply of such works. They were thus instrumental in keeping Hanafism viable in Egypt, a province in which officials of the Ottoman government and provincial grandees tended to be Hanafi but in which the Shafi'i and Maliki rites were dominant. A new post, that of Shaykh al-Azhar, or rector of the university, emerged sometime in the late seventeenth century and was monopolized first by Malikis, then, after 1788, by Shafi'is. To this day, no Hanafi has ever held this position, which by the time of the 1798 French invasion of Egypt was one of the most influential religious offices in Egypt, along with that of head of the descendants of the Prophet Muhammad. By this time, in any case, the office of head of the Prophet's descendants had been taken over by Cairo's two leading families of Prophetic descendants, both of whom were Shafi'i; it was no longer the preserve of Turcophone Hanafis from Istanbul.

FOUNDATIONS

During his thirty-year tenure as chief harem eunuch, Beshir Agha commissioned pious and/or charitable foundations throughout the Ottoman Empire. Here, I focus on his mosque within the Topkapı Palace compound; his religious complex near Topkapı Palace; his school for the study of Prophetic traditions at the Eyüp cemetery; his Qur'an school over a fountain in Cairo; theological colleges connected with Beshir Agha, notably that of Mahmud I in Cairo; and various fountains.

Mosque in Topkapı Palace

Just outside the harem walls, at the far western side of the Second Court of Topkapı Palace, Beshir Agha commissioned a small mosque, perhaps during the 1730s. Anyone with the requisite wealth might commission a small mosque for daily prayer; in contrast, only an imperial official could commission a large mosque in which the communal Friday noontime prayer was held. Beshir's mosque was entirely separate from the smaller mosque inside the harem compound typically used by the rank and file of palace eunuchs. In his book *The Harem*, which surveys the palace in the early years of the Turkish Republic, as it was being converted into a museum, N. M. Penzer describes Beshir's mosque as a ruin. During the 1940s, however, it was restored. Like Beshir's religious complex, his palace mosque is built of red brick and white stone in a baroque style.

Religious complex near Topkapı Palace

A complex of this sort typically consisted of a theological college, a mosque large enough to accommodate the Friday public prayer service, and often a sufi lodge in which a particular mystical order held its distinguishing spiritual ritual. Beshir Agha's complex, located just west of Topkapı Palace in the neighborhood known today as Cağaloğlu, contained all these elements, as well as a library, or book depot, and a fountain. It is a smallish compound built of red brick and white stone in a style that is very subtly baroque; in this respect it resembles the mosque commissioned by Ahmed III's mother and Beshir's sometime ally, Gülnush Emetullah, on the Asian shore of the Bosphorus. In recent years, the mosque and the long courtyard fronting it have been restored. On the southern side of the prayer hall inside the mosque is a double door, over which is a small metal cartouche reading, in Arabic, "There are books inside it." The long, narrow room behind the door remains unrestored, in striking contrast to the prayer hall, and is today in a rather parlous state, virtually empty but for peeling plaster and dust. Here, we must surmise, were stored the 1007 volumes described above.

The theological college, which lies to the south of the courtyard, contains twelve chambers for students. The sufi lodge, set a bit apart at the rear of the complex, during the 1990s housed a foundation supporting Muslim refugees from northeastern Greece. Between its construction in 1745 and the westernizing reforms that the Ottomans undertook in the 1820s, the lodge comprised dervish cells for both men and women, a kitchen and refectory, and a hall in which the communal mystical ritual by which a sufi order is distinguished might be performed. Sufi tendencies appear to have been rather common among harem eunuchs, as witness the many manuscripts of works by famous sufi authors through the ages in the libraries of both Beshir Agha and his seventeenth-century predecessor Abbas Agha. This was not, moreover, the only sufi lodge that Beshir Agha commissioned.

Although the lodge was used by the conservative Naqshbandi sufi order after the westernizing reforms of the 1820s, to what sufi order Beshir himself might have been attached remains unclear. To judge from an inscription that he added to the mausoleum of a prominent Khalwati sufi shaykh in a working-class neighborhood of Istanbul, however, we can deduce that he had ties to the Khalwatis, who indeed were quite widespread in both the Ottoman central lands and the Arab provinces during his lifetime. In Cairo, in fact, the Khalwatis were embarking on a period of unprecedented efflorescence and influence toward the end of Beshir Agha's life, by which time most scholars connected with al-Azhar university were also prominent Khalwatis. The fact that the Khalwati order, a rather diffuse order whose branches were autonomous one from the other, linked the Ottoman central territories to the Arab lands made it practically ideal for chief eunuchs of the imperial harem. On the other hand, the manuscripts formerly housed in the book depot in the nearby mosque include works by authors of a variety of sufi orders. The chief eunuch may have been initiated into several orders, or at least may have attended the rituals of several, as was the practice of many Muslim scholars during the eighteenth century.

At the northeast corner of Beshir Agha's complex is a poorly preserved drinking fountain – today used as a concession stand for snacks and soft drinks, as are many such fountains located at the external corners of such complexes. The restored mosque also has a functioning ablution fountain for worshipers. At the southeast corner, next to the rear wall of the library, a covered staircase provides a sort of back entrance into the complex. This may well have been used by Beshir Agha himself.

School of Prophetic traditions at Eyüp

Eyüp is a neighborhood outside Istanbul's Byzantine land walls, dominated by the sprawling cemetery where Beshir Agha and many other Ottoman officials are buried. As noted above, he endowed a small library there. He also apparently founded a school for the study of the oral traditions of the Prophet Muhammad. No doubt the school made use of his library of theological works, which would have been entirely germane to its purpose. No trace remains of this school, nor do we know anything about the students trained there.

Sabil-Kuttab *in Cairo*

As noted in chapter 5, Beshir Agha's *sabil-kuttab*, or Qur'an school over a fountain, in Cairo was built under the supervision of his agent, or *wakil*, Hasan Agha. This sort of structure was already well known in Cairo. The later Mamluk sultans had incorporated *sabil-kuttab*s into their own architectural foundations, as witness the spectacular example at the corner of the caravanserai commissioned by one of the last Mamluk sultans in the early sixteenth century; this structure stands near al-Azhar and Cairo's most famous bazaar. During the seventeenth century, governors of Egypt began to commission free-standing *sabil-kuttab*s, unconnected to any larger religious or commercial complexes. By the eighteenth century, the *sabil-kuttab* had become the most common structure commissioned by Egypt's provincial notables, whether transplants from the imperial capital or locals. One reason for this was no doubt the far lower cost of constructing and maintaining a one-room Qur'an school and fountain, as opposed to a mosque, to say nothing of a ponderous complex complete with theological college, soup kitchen, and other facilities.

In Cairo, furthermore, *sabil-kuttab*s fit far more readily into existing urban configurations. As the architectural historian Ülkü Bates has shown (Bates 1991, p. 142), early Ottoman governors of Egypt preferred to build on relatively unoccupied, elevated ground so that their mosques would achieve the visual force of their counterparts in Istanbul, Edirne, and the early Ottoman capital of Bursa, southeast of Istanbul. The free-standing *sabil-kuttab*, in contrast, by its very nature complemented pre-existing structures. Thus, the *sabil-kuttab* of Sitt Nafisa, wife of the rebellious eighteenth-century Egyptian grandee Ali Bey (mentioned in chapter 9), stands just south of the southern gate of the original tenth-century city of Cairo and meshes architecturally with the gate itself and with the fifteenth-century Mamluk sultanate mosque whose ornate minarets soar over the two posts of the gate.

The endowment deed of Beshir Agha's *sabil-kuttab*, published by Hamza Abd al-Aziz Badr and Daniel Crecelius, provides clues to the motivation behind this foundation. This document specifies that the revenues accruing to the foundation were to support a Hanafi "jurisprudent," a term which in Arabic typically refers to an expert in religious law but which can, and here probably does, refer to a simple Qur'an-school instructor. The fact that this instructor, by the terms of the foundation, must be Hanafi is significant in the context of Cairo, where the dominant Sunni legal rites were Shafi'i and Maliki. These schools of legal thought differed primarily in details of ritual and in interpretation of personal status matters such as divorce and inheritance. Nonetheless, the Hanafi rite was the official Ottoman rite and, as such, was highly visible publicly in the empire's European provinces, as well as Anatolia and, to some extent, Syria. Egypt, however, was the birthplace of the Shafi'i rite; the founder of that rite is himself buried in Cairo. Meanwhile, the inhabitants of Upper Egypt, like those of North Africa, had historically adhered to the Maliki rite.

Although the later Mamluk sultans had followed the Hanafi rite themselves and patronized Hanafi scholars, they had never established Hanafism as any sort of official rite. The Ottomans, however, appointed a Hanafi chief judge and, until the eighteenth century, a Hanafi chief of the community of descendants of the Prophet Muhammad in every major province. Even provincial grandees in

Egypt made charitable contributions to, or even founded, residential colleges of the ancient al-Azhar university that were predominantly Hanafi, notably those of the Turks (Anatolians) and Indians (while southern Indians were likely to be Shafi'i, northerners were usually Hanafi). In assigning a Hanafi teacher to his Qur'an school, Beshir Agha was reinforcing the Hanafi presence in Cairo. More specifically, his endowment deed stipulates that the school should offer free education to orphans; in this way, it made Hanafism readily available to boys without familial ties to any other legal rite.

It is certainly worth noting that Beshir Agha's successor as chief harem eunuch, Moralı Beshir Agha, built a slightly more elaborate *sabil-kuttab* directly across from that of el-Hajj Beshir in 1750–1, just after supervising the construction of the theological college of Sultan Mahmud I (discussed below) nearby. This section of Cairo was thus marked as a site of palace-sanctioned Ottoman Hanafism.

Theological college in Bulgaria

Beshir Agha's educational foundations were not limited to Istanbul and Cairo. He also founded a theological college in Sistova (today Shishtov), located on the Danube River on what is today Bulgaria's border with Romania. This college, naturally, followed the Hanafi rite, which was virtually the sole rite represented in the Ottoman Balkans. Beshir Agha's objective, however, was not simply to increase the number of Hanafi institutions in the Ottoman domains but to reinforce the presence of official Ottoman Hanafism and the accompanying official Ottoman religious sanction. During the eighteenth century, a period when the wealth and influence of provincial grandees were increasingly visible and decisive, this assertion of imperial prerogative was symbolically important.

Theological college of Mahmud I in Cairo

Such an agenda may have lain behind an unusually ambitious foundation in Cairo: the theological college of Sultan Mahmud I (r. 1730–

54), constructed under the supervision of el-Hajj Beshir's successor, Moralı Beshir Agha, in 1750 in close proximity to el-Hajj Beshir's and his own *sabil-kuttab*s. All three structures were located near the canal (today paved over) that fed into the Nile from the east; by 1750, this district was the westernmost extent of residential settlement in Cairo and the hub of elite residence. The significance of this construction becomes apparent when we consider that no sultanic theological college had been erected in Cairo since the grandiose foundations of the late Mamluk sultans. For a sitting chief eunuch to supervise construction from Istanbul was likewise extraordinary. This was a time, furthermore, when Egypt's provincial grandees, above all those of the increasingly prominent Qazdağlı household (discussed in chapters 6 and 9), were themselves founding mosques, theological colleges, and sufi lodges while making lavish contributions to al-Azhar. In this context, Mahmud's college seems almost a riposte to these monuments of provincial grandees.

As it exists today, the theological college of Mahmud I is a somewhat austere building of dark stone, obviously erected by local builders, featuring the ziggurat-like roof ornaments popular in Egypt since Cairo's founding in the tenth century, as well as the recessed arches that would later, in the 1770s, come to be associated with the foundations of the Qazdağlı household. Of particular note are the seal of Mahmud I above each window, and the *sabil-kuttab* at the corner of the complex. Here, the *sabil*, or fountain, features a broad, bowed front, while the *kuttab*, or Qur'an school, is polygonal; this new style, also evident in Moralı Beshir's own *sabil-kuttab* nearby, set a precedent in Cairo and would be adopted by, for example, the architects who worked for the Qazdağlı household later in the century. Despite the expense obviously lavished on it, Mahmud's theological college does not seem to have been particularly influential intellectually; it never competed for Hanafi students with al-Azhar, for example.

Fountains

Finally, Beshir Agha commissioned simple water fountains for drinking and washing before prayer, unconnected to Qur'an schools.

Two of these can be found in two neighborhoods in the far north of modern-day Istanbul, on the European side of the Bosphorus. During Beshir Agha's lifetime, these districts were villages separate from Istanbul proper. Such residents as there were would have been largely Greek-speaking Orthodox Christians. Nevertheless, these northerly districts were popular excursion places for members of the Ottoman court, and it was perhaps in this context that Beshir chose to establish fountains there. To provide clean water for ritual ablutions was considered a pious act, while clean running water was especially important to Hanafis, whose distinguishing public trait was their insistence on running water for ablutions before prayer (indeed, the Arabic word for "faucet," *hanafiyya*, derives from this insistence). Here again, then, Beshir Agha was using the pious endowment to erect structures that would underline the Hanafi Muslim presence in the Ottoman domains.

CONCLUSION

In all his foundations, as in his libraries, Beshir Agha proved himself a committed Ottoman Hanafi dedicated to reinforcing the presence of the official Ottoman legal rite throughout the empire. At the same time, the structures he commissioned and the books he collected reveal a man of some degree of spiritual and intellectual complexity: a sometime mystic with a genuine devotion to the Prophet Muhammad and his traditions; a multilingual reader with a keen interest in history, literature, and contemporary theological debates. Shaped by both the palace school and his varied experiences in Cairo and Medina, Beshir Agha through his endowments brought these influences to bear on religious and intellectual life throughout the Ottoman domains.

11

BESHIR AGHA'S DEATH AND BURIAL

Beshir Agha died on 3 June 1746 in his quarters in the harem of Topkapı Palace. He was by this time in his 90s, and his state of mind is unknown. At such an age, a harem eunuch must have resembled a living fossil; his voice would have been unusually high and cracked with age. As noted in chapter 3, Chinese sources refer to elderly eunuchs of the imperial palace in Beijing as sounding like "screaming old women." Premature wrinkling of the skin was a symptom that eunuchs could expect to experience in early adulthood; by the time of his death, therefore, Beshir must have been very wrinkled indeed. The combination of wizened features and high, strident voice must have made him an intimidating presence. At the same time, elderly eunuchs were also observed to suffer frequently from senility, so that we may justifiably ask whether Beshir was fully in control of harem affairs, to say nothing of matters associated with the Holy Cities foundations, during the last decade or so of his life. The responsibilities of his agent Osman Agha in Cairo may have been even weightier than at first appears.

FUNERAL AND BURIAL

The ancient eunuch's death would have reached Sultan Mahmud I's ears by way of one of the subordinate harem eunuchs; at the same time, this person would undoubtedly have informed the sultan's favorite concubine (his mother, a concubine of Mustafa II, had died in 1739). Funeral procedures would have followed the official Hanafi legal rite. Beshir's body would have been washed either by low-ranking harem eunuchs or by professional washers, wrapped in a shroud, and placed in an ornamental coffin for transport to a mosque for prayers, then to the tomb he had prepared in the vast, ancient cemetery at Eyüp. Prayers may well have been said either at the harem eunuchs' mosque inside the harem compound, at Beshir Agha's own mosque just outside the compound, or even at the mosque attached to his complex outside the palace walls. In the last case, a funeral cortège, including the sultan's favorite and other harem women, as well as numerous palace eunuchs, would have gone out the great gate at the entrance to the Second Court and turned right, toward his mosque. From there, the procession, almost surely minus the women and eunuchs, would have continued along the ancient Byzantine processional route to the nearest gate in the old Byzantine land walls, then out the gate to the mosque at Eyüp Sultan, built by Sultan Mehmed II on the purported site where the Prophet Muhammad's standard bearer, Abu Ayyub al-Ansari (Ebu Eyüp in Turkish rendering; the name Ayyub is equivalent to the biblical Job), had fallen in battle against the Byzantines.

Outside the mosque was (and is) a vast cemetery where numerous sultans, palace officials, scholar-officials, and other dignitaries have been buried over the centuries. It was an honorable and even prestigious site for burial, befitting Beshir's lengthy tenure and service. Here, the eunuch's shrouded body would have been removed from the coffin while the prayer "Peace on the family of the Messenger of God" was recited by the officiating prayer-leader, and placed on its right side in the grave, with the head facing in the direction of Mecca. The *Fatiha*, the opening chapter of the Qur'an, was surely recited; although some earlier Hanafi jurists disapproved of this practice, it was so widespread under the Ottomans that "The *Fatiha* was read" was frequently inscribed on tombstones. Someone close to Beshir – perhaps a client or even his chosen successor, Moralı Beshir Agha – would have whispered the Muslim profession of faith in the corpse's ear, so that the deceased would be better prepared to answer the questions of the two angels who are believed to appear in the grave immediately after burial to interrogate the deceased on his faith. Harem eunuchs apparently took this rite of passage quite seriously. An influential treatise on this interrogation was composed by a seventeenth-century Hanafi jurisprudent; a copy is recorded in the estate inventory of the chief eunuch Abbas Agha, who died in Cairo in the late seventeenth century. Official mourning would have lasted for forty days – that is, until 13 July 1746 – after which there would have been additional prayers.

BESHIR AGHA'S TOMB

The tomb of Beshir Agha in the Eyüp cemetery is a relatively humble domed structure overlooking a corner of the courtyard of the mosque of Abu Ayyub al-Ansari, for whom the cemetery is named. A fountain graces the tomb courtyard. The inscription over the entrance to the tomb reads:

> The former support of the Abode of Felicity [the harem],
> Beshir Agha, possessor of virtue, commander of nobility,
> Lies here. For many years, with his acts of generosity, which were the most brilliant adornment of the seat of power,
> He behaved as a slave to the summons to prayer.
> When he left the world, His Excellency found another high position.
> For when he realized that the happiness of the world was not everlasting,
> See the sincerity with which he set out on his final journey.
> A halting place was made for him in the vicinity of Khalid [i.e., Abu Ayyub al-Ansari].
> May God forgive his sins.
> May his place be in the paradise of his boon-companions, the men of learning.
>
> (Akakuş 1973, p. 190; Demiriz 1982, pp. 38–9)

The poem's chief metaphorical conceit likens Beshir Agha's life to a long journey, ending in a "halting place." The Ottoman Turkish word used here refers to a waystation where caravans or armies could rest along the route of travel or march. The analogy between a grave and such a halting place is very apt in a Muslim context, since the grave is indeed thought to function as a sort of halting place for the soul while it is interrogated by the two angels. (Christianity also likens the grave to a waystation along the soul's road to salvation or perdition.)

In the inscription, "Khalid" refers to Abu Ayyub al-Ansari himself, whose given name was Khalid. Indeed, Beshir Agha's "halting place" was quite near to that of Abu Ayyub, as noted above, and the poet seems to be making the most of the implications of this physical proximity, perhaps encouraging visitors to the tomb to make a mental link between the late Beshir Agha and the long-deceased standard-bearer. Like Abu Ayyub, Beshir was a convert to Islam who embraced his new faith whole-heartedly. The "standards" he bore, however, were the pious endowments he founded, and perhaps above all his libraries, including the one at the Eyüp cemetery itself, which featured a large number of collections of the Prophet's sayings. As chief tomb eunuch, furthermore, Beshir had acted as one of the "helpers" (*ansar* in Arabic, root of the sobriquet al-Ansari) to the Prophet in Medina, just like Abu Ayyub, who had welcomed the Prophet to Medina in 622 C.E.

12

BESHIR AGHA'S LEGACY THROUGH THE LENS OF OTTOMAN "DECLINE"

Beshir Agha occupied the office of chief harem eunuch for a longer period – thirty years – than any other Ottoman chief eunuch before or since. During this time he arguably wielded more influence than any other chief eunuch. He brought the office to the very pinnacle of its political and economic influence, making the chief eunuch the principal force in the education of Ottoman princes and thus in the shaping of Ottoman sultans. By the early eighteenth century, the grand vizier had virtually displaced the sultan as the Ottoman Empire's prime decision-maker – military, political, and even economic – yet Beshir emerged as the chief force in selecting, patronizing, and deposing grand viziers as well. In short, Beshir Agha became, for all practical purposes, the most powerful single figure in the entire Ottoman Empire, even if the grand vizier continued to be the empire's public face.

MORALI BESHIR AGHA

The very fact that el-Hajj Beshir was followed by no fewer than four other chief eunuchs named Beshir testifies to his unprecedented influence. Clearly, his first name had become a popular eunuch name, perhaps in the expectation that it would bring good fortune to eunuchs who bore it. Unfortunately, the name did not suffice to save el-Hajj Beshir's immediate successor, Moralı Beshir Agha, from his own poor judgment. According to an eighteenth-century Ottoman statesman who wrote a compendium of chief eunuch biographies culminating in Moralı Beshir, the latter surrounded himself with a veritable praetorian guard of mamluks from the Nogay Tatar tribes, who lived north of the Crimean peninsula and were typically known as raiders who acquired mamluks for others, not as mamluks themselves. These Nogay mamluks wrought havoc in Istanbul; public alarm at their brutality triggered Moralı Beshir Agha's execution after he was imprisoned in the "Maiden's Tower" (a.k.a. Leander's Tower), a tiny island prison at the confluence of the Bosphorus and the Sea of Marmara, for several days. His execution would have been of the type reserved for palace insiders and similar servants of the sultan, as opposed to rebels and enemy warlords: he would almost certainly have been strangled in secrecy rather than publicly executed by beheading or, as was most common at the time, hanging. Neither his head nor his body would have been publicly exposed. Regardless, he became one of the very, very few palace eunuchs ever to be executed; such a fate was extraordinary indeed, and intensely shameful. He was buried on the Asian side of the Bosphorus in a cemetery for harem eunuchs of relatively little distinction.

CHIEF HAREM EUNUCHS AND GRAND VIZIERS IN THE POST-BESHIR ERA

Although Moralı Beshir's fate was anomalous, it did signal an emerging challenge to the chief harem eunuch's influence following el-Hajj Beshir's death – a challenge prompted by the unprecedented extent of his powers. The grand viziers during the period after el-Hajj Beshir's death were, of course, aware of the precedent he had set, and several of them determined to subvert this pattern, in some cases by opposing the chief eunuch more or less openly. Perhaps the most graphic example of such a confrontation between a grand vizier and a chief eunuch was that between Raghib Mehmed Pasha, who was grand vizier from 1757 to 1763, and the chief eunuch Ebukoff Ahmed Agha (term 1754–7). This rivalry lay behind the appointment of Husayn ibn al-Makki as governor of Damascus and the subsequent pilgrimage caravan disaster in 1757, covered in chapter 9, for Ibn al-Makki was a protégé of Ebukoff Ahmed Agha and had used this connection to obtain the governorship, which until then had been the monopoly of Syria's Azm family. Although no friend of the Azms, Raghib Mehmed Pasha was determined to prevent Ebukoff Ahmed Agha and future chief harem eunuchs from deciding such high-level appointments. In this case, Raghib's experience as governor of Egypt during the 1740s, when Beshir Agha's death changed the balance of power among that province's political households, as noted in chapter 9, surely influenced his decision to challenge the authority of the chief eunuch.

Ironically, then, Beshir Agha's longevity in office and the enormous authority that he accumulated in the course of his thirty-year tenure as chief harem eunuch may have made it difficult for succeeding chief eunuchs to follow his example. Chastened by the precedent he had set, grand viziers in the latter half of the eighteenth century, Raghib Mehmed Pasha above all, may well have vowed never again to allow a chief eunuch unilaterally to determine the most important imperial appointments and the course of imperial strategy. Although the Ottoman harem would see a number of influential chief eunuchs right up until the empire's demise following World War I, never again would a single chief eunuch occupy the office for so long a time or exercise such a monopoly on power.

BESHIR AGHA AND THE QUESTION OF OTTOMAN "DECLINE"

Beshir Agha was active during a period that has conventionally been portrayed as the depths of the Ottoman Empire's "decline." Following the reign of Sultan Süleyman I (r. 1520–66), according to the conventional narrative, the Ottoman Empire entered a profound decline that lasted at least until the adoption of westernizing reforms in the nineteenth century and, by some accounts, straight through to the end of the empire in the early twentieth century. This decline was marked by the end of territorial expansion and, beginning in the late seventeenth century, an alarming loss of territory to the Habsburg and Russian Empires. Meanwhile, corruption spread through the Ottoman administrative and military ranks. Socio-economic effects of the onset of decline in the late sixteenth and early seventeenth centuries included galloping inflation, peasant flight from the land, and general lawlessness in the countryside.

Within the past twenty years, however, scholars of the Ottoman Empire have questioned and, ultimately, rejected this narrative of decline. In the first place, 300 years is an extraordinarily long time for an empire to decline; relatively few empires in history have even lasted for 300 years, let alone had the luxury of declining for such a lengthy period. While revisionist historians concede that the empire faced a military, economic, and demographic crisis in the late sixteenth and early seventeenth centuries, they argue that it weathered this crisis and, in so doing, entered a new phase of its lengthy existence: one no longer focused on military conquest and territorial expansion but on shoring up loyalty to the Ottoman dynasty in territories already under Ottoman rule, not least by emphasizing the sultan's role as custodian of the Holy Cities of Mecca and Medina and chief representative of Sunni Islam.

Admittedly, the Ottoman sultan during this new phase of "crisis and adaptation," as it is now called, became a less publicly visible figure. No longer did he lead military campaigns in person or make strategic marriage alliances with foreign princesses. Instead, the sultans during these years kept largely to the palace, either in Istanbul or in Edirne, leaving their grand viziers to fight their wars. Crown princes were no longer sent out to the provinces to learn statecraft but remained in the palace harem. Indeed, the harem grew more crowded during these years, for a new sultan no longer killed off his brothers in order to eliminate potential rivals for the throne. Meanwhile, a series of underage and mentally challenged sultans in the seventeenth century gave the sultans' mothers and other harem personnel, including the harem eunuchs, an unprecedented degree of influence in shaping imperial policy and often in choosing grand viziers.

The chief harem eunuch was, in certain respects, the personification of "decline." As noted in chapter 2, the office originated in the late sixteenth century, just when "decline" is conventionally thought to have set in. Even if we accept the revisionist narrative of an empire that faced and overcame a profound crisis between the late sixteenth and the late seventeenth centuries, the eighteenth century is still widely regarded as a period when decline finally caught up with the Ottoman Empire, despite the legacy of the Köprülü reforms and an upturn in the Ottoman economy. By the eighteenth century, Venice was the only European polity against which Ottoman arms were successful any longer, while quasi-autonomous local potentates dominated the provinces. In this context, the chief harem eunuch appears as the decadent remnant of a defunct system.

Despite it all, however, the Ottoman system continued to function for nearly 200 more years. In 1739, a century before the empire adopted thorough-going Europeanizing reforms, canny Ottoman diplomacy of the sort described in chapter 8 won the empire forty years of peace on the Habsburg front. In the Ottoman provinces, meanwhile, the authority of local notables was offset by the hybrid Ottoman–local political culture they nurtured and their eagerness to maintain good relations with the imperial capital. Indeed, the chief harem eunuch, both in office and after deposition, served as a critical link between Istanbul and the provinces through his patronage of provincial clients. Meanwhile, the requirements of the pious foundations for the Holy Cities, which the chief eunuch supervised and which encompassed endowed land and properties in virtually every Ottoman province, united the empire in a network of financial and religious obligations.

Why, then, did European observers portray the Ottoman Empire of Beshir Agha's day as such a decadent, contemptible entity, a mere shadow of its former glorious self? I suspect that Europeans often did not know quite what to make of the empire at this stage, when it was still a considerable power yet no longer, by any stretch of the imagination, the scourge of Europe, and when the sultan was undeniably a more elusive, secluded figure than he had been in the "glory days" of Süleyman the Magnificent. The inaccessibility to male Europeans of the harem, in which sultans and crown princes now seemed to spend most of their time, made that shadowy domain seem all the more alien and mysterious.

In such a context, the figure of the chief eunuch seems to have struck many Europeans as especially sinister. Historically, the chief eunuch was one of a relatively small circle of favorites who began to cluster around the Ottoman sultan beginning in the late sixteenth century; as such, he was little different from the various favorites or "insiders" of contemporary European courts. Yet most European observers seem unable to get beyond his eunuchhood to make this comparison. After all, Western Europe, as opposed to Eastern Europe and much of Asia and Africa, had very little experience of eunuchs outside of the *castrati* who graced European opera houses during the eighteenth and early nineteenth centuries. The harem eunuch was able to cross gender boundaries unlike any political actor in Western European royal courts. It must have seemed bizarre indeed to European visitors to Topkapı Palace to observe emasculated men – particularly Africans, who were quite unfamiliar and exotic to most Europeans – mediating between male and female harems, filling roles that in Western Europe would have been the exclusive preserve of ladies-in-waiting. These visitors must have found it difficult to imagine that such eunuchs could play a role in shaping and preserving the religious and intellectual culture of such a great empire while maintaining that empire's political viability.

Adding to the negative impressions of such observers was the fact that, since the late sixteenth century, various Ottoman intellectuals had had their own axes to grind against African harem eunuchs, largely because these eunuchs belonged to rival patron–client networks from those to which the intellectuals belonged. Thus, for example, the late sixteenth-century statesman and intellectual Mustafa Ali (1541–1600) inveighed against the African eunuchs whom he encountered during a sojourn in Cairo, at least in part because they threatened the interests of his own patron, the Hungarian eunuch Gazanfer Agha, mentioned in chapter 3. Intellectuals such as Mustafa Ali also wrote treatises bemoaning the state to which the Ottoman Empire had come when African eunuchs and their clients could acquire positions of great prestige and influence, often at the expense of these authors. Such "decline" treatises, composed right up until the first tentative attempts at westernizing reforms at the end of the eighteenth century, confirmed an earlier generation of modern-day scholars of the Ottoman Empire in the opinion that the empire did indeed suffer through an uninterrupted 300-year decline. In this context, the chief harem eunuch loomed large as part of "what went wrong." But just as the "decline" paradigm has been revised in favor of a more balanced scheme of crisis and adaptation, so the image of the chief harem eunuch must be revised from that of debauched personification of Ottoman decadence to agent of this adaptation. This is one purpose of the present book.

CONCLUSION

Beshir Agha's life story is that of an Abyssinian slave who became the most powerful person in the Ottoman Empire. One of thousands of Abyssinian boys swept up in the brutal swirl of the sub-Saharan slave trade, castrated in Upper Egypt, sold in Cairo, then brought to Topkapı Palace, Beshir Agha became one of the rare few who not only survived these wrenching violations and displacements but came to transcend them and, ultimately, to prosper beyond the wildest dreams of anyone in his family of origin. His experience was shared by only a tiny minority even among the vast numbers of the "sultan's servants," whether recruits of the *devshirme*, the distinctively Ottoman system of "collection," from the Balkans or purchased slaves from the Caucasus or eastern Africa.

In addition to exerting a profound influence on Ottoman court culture, provincial political culture, and imperial policy (including foreign relations) that would persist long after his death, Beshir Agha played a key role in molding officially sanctioned Ottoman Sunni Islam. Through his superintendency of the imperial pious foundations for the Holy Cities, as well as through his service as chief of the eunuchs who guarded the Prophet Muhammad's tomb in Medina, he left his mark on the manner in which the pilgrimage to the Holy Cities and veneration of the Prophet were carried out under the Ottomans. By sponsoring libraries, Qur'an schools, and more advanced theological colleges at critical locations throughout the empire, furthermore, Beshir Agha ensured the vitality of the official Hanafi legal rite.

Of arguably equal importance was his active patronage of sufi orders and the structures in which they practiced their rituals at a time when these orders were still recovering from the virulent attacks of the puritanical Kadızadeli movement during the late seventeenth century. The efflorescence of the Khalwati and Naqshbandi orders in the Arab lands, above all, during the eighteenth century, while it would certainly have occurred without Beshir Agha's intervention, was unquestionably reinforced by his contributions. A key tendency of this invigorated eighteenth-century sufism, emulation of the Prophet Muhammad's example through intensified recourse to his tradition, benefited greatly from Beshir Agha's widespread promotion of study of the Prophet's sayings, and provision of collections of and commentaries on these sayings in his numerous libraries. This emasculated Abyssinian slave, by the end of his extraordinarily long life, had left his mark as a Sunni Muslim adept, statesman, man of letters, mystic, and bibliophile.

13

SOURCES ON BESHIR AGHA

PRIMARY SOURCES

On the Ottoman palace and harem

Surprisingly, given the scope of Beshir Agha's influence, to say nothing of his sheer longevity, there are few European-language primary sources dealing specifically with him. Sir Paul Rycaut's *The Present State of the Ottoman Empire* (London, 1668; reprint New York, 1971) contains revealing sections on palace institutions, including a substantial passage on the African harem eunuchs. An earlier description of the Ottoman palace was composed by the Frenchman Nicolas de Nicolay (1517–83), who was attached to the French ambassador; his account was published in Lyon in 1576 as *Les navigations, peregrinations et voyages, faicts* [*sic*] *en la Turquie*; an English version (*The navigations, peregrinations and voyages, made into Turkie*) was published in London in 1585. A modern French edition has now been published under the title *Dans l'empire de Soliman le Magnifique: Nicolas de Nicolay*, edited and annotated by Marie-Christine Gomez-Géraud and Stephane Yérasimos (Paris, 1989). The Venetian ambassador Ottaviano Bon (1552–1623) left what is perhaps the most comprehensive description of the palace and harem composed by a European before the twentieth century; a modern English version of this valuable work has been published as *The Sultan's Seraglio: An Intimate Portrait of Life at the Ottoman Court*, introduced and annotated by Godfrey Goodwin (from the seventeenth-century edition of John [i.e. Robert] Withers; London, 1996). The French merchant Jean-Claude Flachat (d. 1775) served as commercial agent to the harem during the tenure of el-Hajj Beshir's successor, Moralı Beshir Agha, to whom Flachat became close. Flachat's two-volume opus *Observations sur le commerce et sur les arts d'une partie de l'Europe, de l'Asie, de l'Afrique et même des Indes orientales* (Lyon, 1766) contains valuable insights into the chief eunuch's office, along with abundant information pertaining specifically to Moralı Beshir, including the circumstances behind his downfall and execution in 1752.

For those who read Ottoman Turkish, Mehmed Süreyya Bey's (1845–1909) *Sicill-i Osmani* contains a brief capsule biography of Beshir Agha; it is available in two Arabic-script editions (Ankara, 1969, and Westmead, Farnborough, England, 1971) and one Roman-alphabet edition (ed. Ali Aktan; Istanbul, 1995). Ahmed Resmi Efendi's (1700–83) *Hamîlet ül-kübera'* (*The Ostrich Plumes of the Great*) is a compendium of more substantial chief harem eunuch biographies, running through Moralı Beshir Agha. The Ottoman Turkish text has now been published in facsimile, along with a Roman-alphabet transcription (ed. Ahmet Nezihi Turan; Istanbul, 2000).

The late nineteenth-century catalogue of the library attached to Beshir's religious complex outside the palace was published on its completion as *Defter-i Kütüphane-i Beşir Ağa[-yı] İstanbul'da Bâb-i Âlî Civarında Vâki'dir* (*Register of the Library of Beshir Agha Located in the Vicinity of the Sublime Porte in Istanbul*) (Istanbul, 1886). Meanwhile, the foundation deed of Gülnush Emetullah's 1678 pious endowment for Mecca has been published in a modern Turkish edition in the collection *Tarihimizde Vakıf Kuran Kadınlar: Hanım Sultan Vakfiyyeleri* (*Pious Endowment-Founding Women in our History: Foundation Deeds of Imperial Women*), ed. Tülay Duran (Istanbul, 1990).

The Book of Festivals

The 1720 *Book of Festivals* by the court chronicler Vehbi, with illustrations by the court painter Levni, including several depictions of Beshir Agha and various other harem and threshold eunuchs, has now been published in an English edition: *Levni and the Sûrnâme: The Story of an Eighteenth-Century Ottoman Festival*, edited with commentary by Esin Atıl (Istanbul, 1999). A second English edition, though without a complete set of illustrations, also exists: *Sûrnâme: An Illustrated Account of Sultan Ahmed III's Festival of 1720*, ed. Ahmet Ertuğ (Berne, 2000).

On the East African slave trade

European sources dealing with the procurement of young African eunuchs for palace service, including the castration procedure, include John Lewis Burckhardt's (1784–1817) two-volume *Notes on the Bedouins and the Wahabys, Collected during His Travels in the East* (London, 1831). More general information on Beshir's native land can be found in Burckhardt's *Travels in Nubia* (London, 1819). Sir Richard Francis Burton (1821–90) supplies details of the degrees of castration in his legendary translation of *The 1001 Nights: The Book of the Thousand Nights and a Night: A Plain and Literal Translation of the Arabian Nights Entertainments*, of which countless editions exist. A more concise account of the slave trade and castration can be found in the memoir of the French physician Louis Franck (1761–1825), *Mémoire sur le commerce des nègres au Kaire [sic], et sur les maladies auxquelles ils sont sujets en y arrivant*, translated into English by Michel Le Gall and published in Shaun E. Marmon (ed.), *Slavery in the Islamic Middle East* (Princeton, 1999).

On the Arab provinces

A detailed and extremely valuable source on the Prophet's mosque and tomb in Medina, as well as the role of the eunuchs who guarded the Prophet's tomb, is Richard Francis Burton's *Personal Narrative of a Pilgrimage to al-Madinah and Meccah* (Memorial edn. London, 1893; republished New York, 1964). Although Burton visited the Holy Cities during the 1850s, many of his observations apply equally to the period when Beshir Agha was active. The first volume of Burton's narrative is devoted largely to Medina, the second largely to Mecca.

Brief, rather cryptic mentions of Beshir Agha and his agents in Cairo appear sporadically in the annalistic chronicle attributed to Ahmed Kethüda Azeban al-Damurdashi, a regimental officer living in Cairo in the first half of the eighteenth century. The chronicle, *Al-Durra al-musāna fī akhbār al-Kināna* (*The Protected Pearl: History of Egypt* [land of the Kinana tribe]) (British Museum, MS Or. 1073-1074) has been published in an occasionally problematic English translation by Daniel Crecelius and Abd al-Wahhab Bakr, under the title *Al-Damurdashi's Chronicle of Egypt, 1688-1755: Al-Durra al-musāna fī akhbār al-Kināna* (Leiden and New York, 1989).

SECONDARY SOURCES

In the secondary scholarly literature, general works on the palace, on slavery, and on eunuchs far outnumber studies devoted to individual eunuchs.

Works on the palace and the harem

The rather enigmatic Anglophone author Norman Mosley Penzer (who was, not coincidentally, a scholar of Burton) scrutinized Topkapı Palace during the 1930s, shortly after it was opened to the public as a museum. His account, *The Harem: An Account of the Institution as it Existed in the Palace of the Turkish Sultans, with a History of the Grand Seraglio from its Foundation to Modern Times* (Philadelphia, 1936; republished New York, 1993), is a valuable guide to the layout of the palace and the functions of its various rooms. The author also devotes one chapter to previous accounts of the palace by European visitors. Penzer makes no attempt to mask his opinion that the palace eunuchs were a debauched and decadent population; although his description of their character and proclivities is shot through with prejudice and outright fantasy, his account of their duties and quarters is extremely useful. Gülru Necipoğlu's *Architecture, Ceremonial, and Power: The Topkapı Palace in the Fifteenth and Sixteenth Centuries* (New York and Cambridge, Mass., 1991) can serve as a more scholarly complement to Penzer's architectural tour of the palace, at least for the earlier period. Likewise, Leslie P. Peirce's *The Imperial Harem: Women and Sovereignty in the Ottoman Empire* (New York and Oxford, 1993) gives a more nuanced and sophisticated view of the functions and authority of the palace women, at the same time placing the harem eunuchs in the context of the women's environment and functions.

A general sense of the part played by the harem women and the chief eunuch in the fortunes of the Ottoman Empire during the early eighteenth century can be gained from Mary Lucille Shay, *The Ottoman Empire from 1720 to 1734, as Revealed in Despatches of the Venetian Baili* (Urbana, Ill., 1944; reprinted Westport, Conn., 1978). Shay reproduces uncritically the often contemptuous observations of the ambassadors to the Ottoman court of the Republic of Venice, which was in the process of losing the last of its empire to the Ottomans at the time. Nonetheless, the work provides useful detail on the grand vizierate of Nevshehirli Ibrahim Pasha and on the Patrona Halil rebellion of 1730, as well as on Beshir Agha's subsequent career as "vizier maker."

The career of the grand vizier Raghib Mehmed Pasha is detailed in Norman Itzkowitz, "Mehmet Raghip Pasha: The Making of an Ottoman Grand Vizier," unpublished Ph.D. dissertation, Princeton University, 1958, and cited in abbreviated form in idem, "Eighteenth-Century Ottoman Realities," *Studia Islamica,* 16 (1962), 73–94. Meanwhile, Karl K. Barbir's *Ottoman Rule in Damascus, 1708–1758* (Princeton, 1980) addresses the hold of the Azm family over that province, as well as the attempts of Fathi Efendi and Husayn ibn al-Makki to dislodge them.

Finally, a section on the institution of palace eunuchs in general, including useful examples drawn from the Chinese empire, can be found in Orlando Patterson, *Slavery and Social Death: A Comparative Study* (Cambridge, Mass., 1982).

Studies of eunuchs under the Mamluk sultanate

By a happy coincidence, we possess two valuable recent studies of eunuchs under the Mamluk sultanate, which ruled Egypt, Syria, southeastern Anatolia, and the western Arabian peninsula (including

Mecca and Medina) from 1250 until the Ottoman conquest of these territories in the early sixteenth century. David Ayalon's *Eunuchs, Caliphs, and Sultans: A Study of Power Relationships* (Jerusalem, 1999) takes a broad look at the use of eunuchs in early and medieval Islamic societies, culminating in a detailed examination of the functions of eunuchs under the Mamluks, particularly their role in educating raw recruits to the mamluk armies. Shaun E. Marmon's *Eunuchs and Sacred Boundaries in Islamic Society* (Oxford and New York, 1995) is the only secondary study to date of the eunuchs who guarded the Prophet Muhammad's tomb in Medina. The author examines in some detail the purported origins of this institution, then places it in the context of Mamluk sultanate political and religious strategy. Many of her observations are pertinent to the Ottoman period as well. Marmon's study can be supplemented by Suraiya Faroqhi's valuable *Pilgrims and Sultans: The Hajj under the Ottomans* (London and New York, 1994), which offers additional information on Ottoman-era Medina.

Studies of Beshir Agha and other eunuchs in Ottoman Cairo

A number of articles and book chapters deal with the economic – and, to some extent, political – activities of Beshir Agha and of various exiled Ottoman harem eunuchs in Cairo. Of particular note is Hamza Abd al-Aziz Badr and Daniel Crecelius, "The *Awqāf* [pious endowments] of al-Hajj Bashir Agha in Cairo," *Annales Islamologiques,* 27 (1993), 291–311, which includes a transcription and translation of the foundation deed for Beshir Agha's *sabil-kuttab*, along with photographs of the structure. The same two authors have published a similar article dealing with the pious endowments of a seventeenth-century harem eunuch (never chief eunuch, however) named Shahin Ahmed Agha: "The *Waqf* [pious endowment] of Shahin Ahmad Agha in Cairo," *Annales Islamologiques,* 26 (1992). My own "The Wealth and Influence of an Exiled Ottoman Eunuch in Egypt: The *Waqf* [pious endowment] Inventory of Abbas Agha," *Journal of the Economic and Social History of the Orient,* 37/4 (1994), 293-317, scrutinizes the estate inventory of a chief harem eunuch exiled to Cairo in 1671.

Meanwhile, my "The Role of the Kızlar Ağası [chief harem eunuch] in 17th–18th Century Ottoman Egypt," *Studia Islamica,* 75 (1992), 141–58, describes the role of exiled harem eunuchs in Egypt in more general terms, while my book *The Politics of Households in Ottoman Egypt: The Rise of the Qazdağlıs* (Cambridge, 1997) contains a chapter on the relations of Egypt's Qazdağlı household, which dominated the province for much of the eighteenth century, with various chief eunuchs, exiled and otherwise, including Beshir. Finally, my recent article "Exiled Chief Harem Eunuchs as Proponents of the Hanafi *Madhhab* [Sunni legal rite] in Ottoman Cairo," *Annales Islamologiques,* 37 (2003), 191–9, takes up the religio-intellectual influence of exiled chief harem eunuchs, Beshir Agha above all.

Sources on Beshir Agha's tomb

Lastly, the tomb of Beshir Agha in Istanbul's Eyüp cemetery is described in two Turkish works: Recep Akakuş's *Eyyüp Sultan ve Mukaddes Emanetler* (*Eyüp Sultan [Cemetery] and Holy Trusts*) (Istanbul, 1973), and Yıldız Demiriz's *Eyüp'te Türbeler* (*Tombs in Eyüp [Cemetery]*) (Ankara, 1982). Both books include the tomb inscription, and the first includes a not terribly revealing photograph of the tomb.

WORKS CITED

PRIMARY SOURCES

Burckhardt, John Lewis. 1831. *Notes on the Bedouins and the Wahabys, Collected during His Travels in the East.* 2 vols. London: John Murray.

Burton, Sir Richard Francis. 1893. *Personal Narrative of a Pilgrimage to al-Madinah and Meccah.* Memorial edn. 2 vols. London: Tylston & Edwards. Republished New York: Dover Publications, 1964.

Damurdashi, Ahmed Kethüda Azeban al-. c.1755. *Al-Durra al-musāna fī akhbār al-Kināna (The Protected Pearl: History of Egypt* [land of the Kinana tribe]). British Museum, MS Or. 1073–1074.

Flachat, Jean-Claude. 1766. *Observations sur le commerce et sur les arts d'une partie de l'Europe, de l'Asie, de l'Afrique et même des Indes orientales.* Lyon: Chez Jacquenod père et Rusand.

Franck, Louis. 1802. *Mémoire sur le commerce des nègres au Kaire* [sic], *et sur les maladies auxquelles ils sont sujets en y arrivant,* trans. Michel Le Gall as "Memoir on the Traffic in Negroes to Cairo and on the Illnesses to which they are Subject upon Arrival There," in Shaun E. Marmon (ed.), *Slavery in the Islamic Middle East.* Princeton: Markus Wiener Publishers, 1999.

Mustafa Ali. 1975. *Mustafa Ali's Description of Cairo of 1599: Text, Transliteration, Translation, Notes,* ed. and trans. Andreas Tietze. Vienna: Österreichische Akademie der Wissenschaften.

Rycaut, Paul. 1668. *The Present State of the Ottoman Empire.* London: John Starkey & Henry Brome. Reprint New York: Arno Press, 1971.

Süreyya, Mehmed. 1971. *Sicill-i Osmani.* 4 vols. Westmead, Farnborough, England: Gregg International Publishers.

SECONDARY SOURCES

Akakuş, Recep. 1973. *Eyyüp Sultan ve Mukaddes Emanetler* (*Eyüp Sultan [Cemetery] and Holy Trusts*). Istanbul: Fatih Yayınevi.

Ayalon, David. 1999. *Eunuchs, Caliphs, and Sultans: A Study of Power Relationships*. Jerusalem: Magnes Press, the Hebrew University.

Badr, Hamza Abd al-Aziz, and Daniel Crecelius. 1993. "The *Awqāf* [pious endowments] of al-Hajj Bashir Agha in Cairo," *Annales Islamologiques*, 27: 291–311.

Bates, Ülkü. 1991. "Façades in Ottoman Cairo," in Irene A. Bierman, Rifa'at A. Abou-El-Haj, and Donald Preziosi (eds.), *The Ottoman City and its Parts: Urban Structure and Social Order*. New Rochelle, NY: Aristide D. Caratzas, pp. 129–71.

Demiriz, Yıldız. 1982. *Eyüp'te Türbeler* (*Tombs in Eyüp [Cemetery]*). Ankara: Turkish Ministry of Culture.

Itzkowitz, Norman. 1962. "Eighteenth-Century Ottoman Realities," *Studia Islamica,* 16: 73–94.

Marmon, Shaun E. 1995. *Eunuchs and Sacred Boundaries in Islamic Society*. New York and Oxford: Oxford University Press.

Penzer, N. M. 1936. *The Harem: An Account of the Institution as it Existed in the Palace of the Turkish Sultans, with a History of the Grand Seraglio from its Foundation to Modern Times*. Philadelphia: J. B. Lippincott. Republished New York: Dorset Press, 1993.

INDEX

MAKERS *of the* MUSLIM WORLD

Series Editor: Patricia Crone
Institute for Advanced Study, Princeton

Among the over fifty titles in the series:

Ibn 'Arabi
William C. Chittick
Renowned expert William Chittick surveys the life and works of this legendary thinker.
ISBN: 1-85168-387-9

Shaykh Mufid
T. Bayhom-Daou
An assessment of the great Shi'ite scholar and theologian.
ISBN: 1-85168-383-6

Abu Nuwas
Philip Kennedy
A readable introduction to this celebrated 9th-century poet.
ISBN: 1-85168-360-7

'Abd al-Malik
Chase F. Robinson
The Umayyad Caliph and founder of the Dome of the Rock is captured in a concise and clear manner.
ISBN: 1-85168-361-5

Fazlallah Astarabadi and the Hurufis
Shahzad Bashir
Discusses the achievements of this Sufi thinker and founder of Gnostic Hurufism.
ISBN: 1-85168-385-2

al-Ma'mun
Michael Cooperson
An introduction to the controversial 9th-century Caliph and patron of the sciences.
ISBN: 1-85168-386-0

Ahmad Riza Khan
Usha Sanyal
On the founder of the 'Barelwi' movement in India in the late 19th/early 20th centuries.
ISBN: 1-85168-359-3

Amir Khusraw
Sunil Sharma
Surveys the life and work of the 14th-century Indian poet, courtier, musician, and Sufi.
ISBN: 1-85168-362-3

'Abd al-Rahman III
Maribel Fierro
Introduces the founder of the great Caliphate of Madinat al-Zahra at Cordova.
ISBN: 1-85168-384-4

Beshir Agha
Jane Hathaway
An examination of the longest serving Chief Harem Eunuch in the history of the Ottoman Empire.
ISBN: 1-85168-390-9

www.oneworld-publications.com